Making Better Decisions About School Problems

This book is dedicated to
Lynne, Ilan, Oren, Mia, Carol, and Nancy

Making Better Decisions About School Problems

How Administrators Use Evaluation to Find Solutions

Naftaly S. Glasman

CORWIN PRESS, INC.
A Sage Publications Company
Thousand Oaks, California

For information address:

Corwin Press, Inc.
A Sage Publications Company
2455 Teller Road
Thousand Oaks, California 91320

SAGE Publications Ltd.
6 Bonhill Street
London EC2A 4PU
United Kingdom

SAGE Publications India Pvt. Ltd.
M-32 Market
Greater Kailash I
New Delhi 110 048 India

Printed in the United States of America

Library of Congress Cataloging-in-Publication Data

Glasman, Naftaly S., 1938-
  Making better decisions about school problems : how administrators use evaluation to find solutions / Naftaly S. Glasman.
      p.   cm.
  Includes bibliographical references and index.
  ISBN 0-8039-6124-3 — ISBN 0-8039-6125-1 (pbk.)
  1. School management and organization—Decision making—Case studies. I. Title.
LB2806.G53   1994
371.2—dc20   93-37725
                                                         CIP

94 95 96 97   10 9 8 7 6 5 4 3 2 1

Corwin Press Production Editor: Rebecca Holland

CONTENTS

List of Tables   vii

List of Figures   viii

Preface   ix

Acknowledgments   xiii

About the Author   xv

1. Two Kinds of Evaluation   1

Introduction   1
Direct Evaluation by Principals   3
Evaluation by Evaluation Professionals   5
Summary   7

2. Problem-Based and Problem-Driven
Decisions and Evaluations   8

Introduction   8
The Model   9
An Illustrative Case of a Problematic Situation   15
An Illustrative Case of a Known Problem   17
A Data Gathering and Analysis Instrument   23
A Test of the Instrument   23
Summary   29

3. Cases of Administrative Use of Evaluation   39

   The Conducting of Administrative Evaluations
      by Elementary School Principals   39
   The Conducting of Administrative Evaluations
      by Middle School Principals   49
   The Conducting of Administrative Evaluations
      by Assistant High School Principals   54
   The Conducting of Administrative Evaluations
      by High School Principals   59

4. Improving Practice: Synthesizing the Cases   64

   Problematic Situations and the Use
      of Administrative Evaluation   65
   Key Decisions and Administrative Use of Evaluation   71
   Additional Considerations About
      Administrative Use of Evaluation Methodologies   85
   Summary   91

5. How the Cases Inform Theory   94

   Evaluation in Administration   94
   Decision-Evaluation Relationships   96
   What Next?   98

6. Practical Applications of the Evaluation Instrument   100

   Introduction   100
   Recording Ongoing Thoughts and Actions   101
   The Use of the Information for Self-Assessment   102
   The Use of the Information for Evaluation
      by the Superordinate   116
   Summary   118

   Resource A: Summary of Cases #11 to #30   120

   References   164

   Index   170

LIST OF TABLES

Table 2.1 Priorities of Problem Owners, Effects of
Problems, and Manageability of Problems
as Evaluation Objects   18

Table 4.1 The 30 Cases by Administrative Domain   66

Table 4.2 Issues or Problems in the Case
of Elementary School Principals   72

Table 4.3 Issues or Problems in the Case
of Middle School Principals   74

Table 4.4 Issues or Problems in the Case
of Assistant High School Principals   75

Table 4.5 Issues or Problems in the Case
of High School Principals   76

Table 4.6 Decisions Made by Elementary School Principals   78

Table 4.7 Decisions Made by Middle School Principals   80

Table 4.8 Decisions Made by Assistant
High School Principals   82

Table 4.9 Decisions Made by High School Principals   83

Table 4.10 The Use of Evaluation Objects
and Evaluation Methodologies as Reported
by 30 School Administrators   87

LIST OF FIGURES

Figure 2.1. Evaluation Instrument   24

Figure 2.2. Evaluation Instrument: A Test   30

Figure 5.1. Decision Making X   96

Figure 5.2. Decision Making Y   97

Figure 6.1. Case #1: An Itinerant Employee   103

Figure 6.2. Case #2: The Curriculum   109

PREFACE

This book is about decisions and evaluations that occur when school administrators find solutions to school problems. To discover and depict these decisions and evaluations, this book incorporates various works, including those about practice, research, and theory. The book begins by using previously reported research and theory to devise a model of problem solving and to test this model with practitioners. The model is then used to produce an instrument that demonstrates how actual practices take place in the form of decisions and evaluations and how these practices can be studied and analyzed. Following this, the instrument is used to examine 30 recent cases of real-life administrative problem solving. The findings of this examination are used for two purposes. One is to enrich the practice of school administration by showing the benefits of engaging in problem solving in ways that include decisions and evaluations more systematic than is customary for administrators. The other purpose is to enrich the scholarly study of school administration by showing the benefits of conceptualizing the problem-solving process as made up primarily of a few internally consistent decisions and several corresponding in-depth evaluations.

One specific central benefit of this book is the "instrument." It is a systematic checklist pertaining to decisions and evaluations that take place when school administrators face problematic situations.

School administrators can use this instrument without help and on their own while they problem solve and examine their perception of their progress against a more objective perspective. Chapter 6 of this book demonstrates how the instrument can be used to record and analyze problematic situations as they unfold and are resolved.

Another central benefit of the book are the 30 cases of real-life problems with real evaluations, real decisions, and real solutions. This real-world research documents evaluation and problem-solving processes of school administrators. It also documents the methods by which school administrators gather their information, consistently using those that involve consideration on one's own, discussion in groups, and discussion with individuals. The research includes examples of solutions others have used for commonly encountered problems. Readers could be easily stimulated in this regard to think about solutions and their adaptation to one's own circumstances. All in all it is possible that to some readers the specific research problem may be of greater interest than the research findings.

Overview of Contents

The first two chapters introduce evaluation as an administrative function at the school level. They also introduce the contexts in which this function exists and serve as a guide in the search of more detailed information.

Chapter 1 draws on two kinds of literature. First it draws on educational administration literature to survey known practices of evaluation by administrators, especially those that are externally mandated to the school and those that the school initiates internally. The chapter identifies authority, control, and politicization as central concepts in these administrative practices. The chapter also draws on educational evaluation literature and focuses on evaluation as practiced by professional evaluators. The chapter emphasizes evaluation of student learning, teacher performance, and educational performance. Evaluation methodologies are mentioned as derivations of the specific evaluation objects. The limited potential of systematized evaluation in administrative work is also noted.

Chapter 2 introduces a new model of the administrative process and a corresponding data collection and analysis instrument. The new model capitalizes on some features of the administrative use of evaluation described in Chapter 1. The model assumes that increased systematization of evaluation in administration is desirable and possible when administrators face major problem situations. The model includes the description of the problematic situation, the delineation of four key decisions that occur during the problem-solving process, and the specification of 22 sets of evaluation scattered among these four decisions. Each of the 22 evaluations includes considerations of the evaluation object ("what is evaluated"), evaluation methodology ("how it is evaluated"), and evaluation findings ("what the evaluation results are"). The instrument is described later in the chapter along with how the instrument was tested as an interview protocol to gather information from school administrators about their decisions and evaluations.

Chapter 3 presents 10 interviews with school administrators using the interview protocol described in Chapter 2. The responses themselves were to the question to describe the problematic situation, the four questions about decisions made, and the 22 sets of questions about the use of evaluation. In total, 30 interviews were conducted with 12 elementary school principals, 6 middle school principals, 6 assistant high school principals, and 6 high school principals. The other 20 cases are summarized in Resource A, to allow readers to sample the array of problem situations identified and to have access to the full range of cases from which the data have been derived.

Chapters 4, 5, and 6 offer different uses of evaluation as part of the problem-driven administrative process. Chapter 4 synthesizes data derived from the 30 interviews for purposes of improved practice. The chapter shows how evaluation helps in describing problematic situations as progressively specific, how information gathered within the evaluative-administrative context increases the consistency among key decisions that are made during the problem-solving process, and how a variety of evaluation methodologies employed in the context of the problem-driven administrative process benefit decision making.

Chapter 5 uses the research data for academic purposes. The research-oriented emphases are on the clarification of some of the characteristics of evaluation itself and the conceptual linkages between evaluations and decisions within the problem-solving and decision-making processes.

Chapter 6 depicts selected practical applications of the instrument that has been developed in this book. The chapter demonstrates how the instrument is used for recording ongoing thoughts and actions associated with specific problematic situations. The chapter also describes the assessments of a school principal and an assistant superintendent about the use of this recording for, respectively, self-evaluation and evaluation by a superordinate.

ACKNOWLEDGMENTS

I acknowledge with respect and joy Gracia Alkema for having encouraged me to take on the project after she heard what it might be. To the 30 school administrators who taught my students and me a solid lesson in school administration, I wish to express my appreciation and gratitude. To my students Robert Arellanes, Doug Bower, Catherine Breen, Deborah Flores, Steve Flores, James Gonzales, and Jana Johnson, who conducted collectively 17 of the 30 interviews for this volume, I wish to express my thanks. Daniel Cooperman and Ida Rickborn made Chapter 6 possible. I thank them sincerely. I also wish to thank Ronald Heck, Gracia Alkema, and Lynne Glasman for reading and commenting on earlier drafts. Lynne has been my greatest English teacher. Finally I am happy to acknowledge Robin Stark and Hildegard Lagerquist who typed the various drafts from beginning to end. The responsibility for the product is mine alone.

Naftaly S. Glasman
University of California, Santa Barbara

ABOUT THE AUTHOR

Naftaly S. (Tuli) Glasman (Ph.D., University of California, Berkeley) has been a member of the faculty of the University of California, Santa Barbara, since 1968. He served as Dean of the Graduate School of Education between 1980 and 1987. He is a former high school teacher (West Hartford, Connecticut) and principal (Oakland, California). He has been a visiting professor in Israel at Ben Gurion University, Haifa University, and Tel Aviv University and is now a visiting professor at UCLA.

Dr. Glasman has written extensively—more than 120 journal articles, book chapters, monographs, and books published in the United States, Israel, Great Britain, Australia, Canada, and Belgium. He was also editor of *Review of Educational Research* and guest editor of *Evaluation Studies* and *Peabody Journal of Education*. His work until 1979 dealt with educational governance and politics, policy-making, administration, and organizations. His work since 1979 has focused on evaluation as an administrative function in education. He has studied input-output relationships in schools, fiscal dimensions of schools, and evaluation of school personnel. He has recently authored *Evaluation-Based Leadership* and coauthored *Evaluation in Decision-Making*. He coedited "New Ways to Assess the Performance of the School Principal" (Parts 1 and 2) in the *Peabody Journal of Education*.

A native of Israel, Dr. Glasman has been a consultant to various governmental and educational agencies in the United States, Israel, and Australia.

1

TWO KINDS OF EVALUATION

Introduction

Pardon the language but the following scene is familiar. It happens many times during the school year in many classrooms where the pertinent school policy is not completely specific. This one occurred in a sixth grade in Palmview School in a Southern California unified school district. It is May of 1992 and Joan raises her hand in class. "Yes, Joan?" asks the teacher, Mrs. Russo.

Joan: May I go to the bathroom again?
Mrs. Russo: It is up to you, Joan. Remember, though, the test is long.
Joan: Okay, I won't go; I don't have to go that badly anyway.

One can see and interpret many things in this short interchange. I see evaluation—the receiving of information and the rendering of judgment about it. Through such spectacles I view both Joan and Mrs. Russo as evaluators. Mrs. Russo's information is Joan's request. Mrs. Russo judges this information and ends up deciding to let Joan know that she can make up her own mind. Mrs. Russo also decides to remind Joan of the length of the test. Now Joan's information is Mrs. Russo's response to her request. Joan judges this information and finally decides to remain in the classroom. As it turns out, Mrs. Russo and Joan are not only evaluators but also decision makers.

How often do Mrs. Russo and Joan evaluate in school? The answer is probably all the time—while talking and while listening, while studying and while playing, and more. Mrs. Russo and Joan are nonprofessional evaluators, however. They probably do not evaluate very systematically. They also most likely do not have a doctorate degree in educational statistics and measurement or in educational psychology, or in educational evaluation, for that matter.

What can they evaluate without being professional evaluators? Probably a lot. They evaluate individuals and tools and places. They evaluate developments and changes and achievement. They evaluate their own and others' thoughts and attitudes, behaviors, and feelings. Consider, for example, how often Mrs. Russo evaluates teaching material before actually teaching it, or how involved she is in evaluating how her new principal deals with parents. Joan evaluates plenty, too—the assignments she gets before doing them, a few girls before she chooses a "best friend," and perhaps her teacher, after they have a short conversation. All of us know, of course, that Brian's decision to telephone Joan followed his judging the information he received in their get-togethers in school that day.

Another evaluator in Joan's school is the school principal. Mrs. Blakely is a nonprofessional evaluator, too. For the purpose of this book, we may label her evaluations and her decisions as "administrative." Mrs. Blakely accepts that she is an evaluator, but her colleague at Adams school, three miles away, does not. Mr. Shoreham sees himself as a decision maker and a problem solver but not as an evaluator, not even when he hears that evaluation may be nothing more than gathering information and judging its worth.

This book is a journey that exposes the reader to the workings of the school principal as an evaluator, whose problem solving is enhanced when framed as an evaluation activity, whether she admits it or not. Chapter 1 starts the reader off on this journey. The roots of this chapter are in 1985, when pressure began to mount to improve school productivity. Three phenomena emerged. One was that school principals consolidated their claim that they (not just professional evaluators) can and do evaluate, too. The second was that professional evaluation expanded and school principals were added to the list of the clients of the evaluation professionals.

Simply put, some principals, with the aid of the district administration, mustered enough money to hire professionals. This went without saying when the project was externally funded. The third phenomenon was that principals' use of rationality increased when they evaluated. There was less ad hoc and more preplanned evaluation behavior (e.g., Glasman, 1986b).

In this chapter the reader is introduced to nonprofessional and professional evaluation in school administration. Both kinds of evaluation add up to what could be labeled as evaluation as an integral administrative function (Glasman, 1979). The first kind of evaluation appears almost everywhere in school administration. The second kind is highly systematic and serves to provide school administrators with what they cannot acquire on their own. It is the consideration of both that gave rise to the ideas to be described in Chapter 2 and the rest of the book.

Direct Evaluation by Principals

To use a metaphor: If administration is like a porous rock on the seashore and problems in administration are like waves, then evaluation is like the ocean water that is absorbed into the pores and exits from them. Evaluation dominates in administration, even though it cannot often be seen. The water is inside the pores, and so is evaluation; it is often inside the thoughts and actions of the administrator, even though unseen.

How many school administrators believe this? Over the last 13 years I have asked over 5,700 school principals in the United States whether they consider themselves evaluators or not. In 1980, about 20% said yes. In 1992, close to 80% said yes. Probably the greatest reason for this increase is the dramatic rise in public demand for educational accountability. Principals have learned that to be known as evaluators enhances the perception that there is accountability in the school.

It is strange that the educational administration literature treats the evaluative function only scantily. Major scholars in the late 1960s mention evaluation only in association with personnel (e.g., Getzels, Lipham, & Campbell, 1968, pp. 332-337). Well-known practitioners in the early 1980s mentioned only a bit more, in that they specified purposes of personnel evaluation (e.g., Stoops, Rafferty, & Johnson, 1981, pp. 380-390). Recent scholars and practitioners go only as far as enumerating a few policies, methodologies, and uses pertinent to personnel evaluation (e.g., Lunenberg & Ornstein, 1991, pp. 481-487).

Yet school administrators have engaged in evaluation extensively over the years. For one thing, they have had to respond in substance to externally mandated demands for evaluation. In the area of vocational education, for example, Public Law 94-482 called for measuring goal achievement and demonstrating the use of evaluation information for improvement (e.g., Campbell, Cunningham, Nystrand, & Usdan, 1980, p. 51). Also, in special education, Public Law 94-142 mandated administration and use of specific tests as well as minimum levels of competence in test administration. State evaluation mandates followed suit (e.g., Glasman, 1982), especially in the nature of information to be collected. The role of state visiting teams has also been spelled out in detail in relation to school administrators (e.g., Borich, 1985). Principals have been found to spend quite a bit of time on these evaluations (e.g., Lacayo, 1992).

School principals have not shown much enthusiasm to engaging in externally mandated evaluation. In most cases they have done just what is required and no more, because such involvement has provided little or no benefits to them (e.g., Alkin, Daillack, & White, 1979; Cousins & Leithwood, 1986). Many of them saw that the mandates would continue (e.g., Bickel & Cooley, 1985), addressing the school districts but targeting the schools (e.g., Glasman & Nevo, 1988). In most cases, districts have negotiated on behalf of the schools with the governmental units that executed the mandates (e.g., Glasman, 1986a).

School administrators have also had to initiate internal evaluations with or without a connection to external mandates. DeRoche (1987) argues that most of these internal efforts have focused on effectiveness. He is probably right. The evaluation questions have included such matters as the effectiveness of the curriculum, teaching and instruction, the school culture and the classroom climate, student activities, personnel services, school community relations, facilities, and more.

The most common system of principal engagement in internally initiated evaluation has been the teacher evaluation plan (e.g., Wise, Darling-Hammond, McLaughlin, & Bernstein, 1984). The role of the principal in this system is usually clear and concise: what to evaluate; for what purpose; and when, how, and what to do with the results (e.g., Webb, Greer, Montello, & Norton, 1987). The data that principals collect may include records of observations, results of competency and mastery tests, self-assessment, and student performance-related records of teacher activities (e.g., Seyfarth, 1991, pp. 206-216). Millman and Darling-Hammond (1990) and Valentine (1992) provide two excellent detailed accounts of several dimensions of teacher evaluation conducted by school principals.

Another common type of evaluation performed by principals is the evaluation of curriculum. In many cases this includes the programs, the medium of instruction, the organization of the material, the teaching strategy, the management of class work, and the role of the teacher (e.g., Lewy, 1977). Oliva (1982) sees curriculum evaluation as much broader than instructional evaluation. McNeil (1990) differentiates between short- and long-term value of curriculum offerings and corresponding evaluations.

How much evaluation authority do school principals have? What and what not do they have authority to evaluate? Very little of the answers to these questions is spelled out in the principals' job description. School principals sometimes are reluctant to embark on an evaluation themselves because they are unclear about their own authorities. This obstacle must be removed. One experiences more difficulties in engaging conscientiously in evaluation when the authority to evaluate is ambiguous than when it is clear. Also, the authority to evaluate is indicative of the overall authority of the principal because administrators exercise control through evaluation.

Evaluation by Evaluation Professionals

As part of the requirements in administering extramural grants or as a response to administrator invitations, professional evaluators design and perform evaluations for school principals and for other school district administrators. In preparation for their work, some professional evaluators begin with constructing or choosing evaluation models that derive from theories, philosophies, or observations of practice (e.g., House, 1980). Others design evaluations without specific models (e.g., Popham, 1974; Thompson, 1980; Patton, 1982).

It was not always so. At the turn of the century, evaluation was synonymous with measurement of student achievement and the latter had little to do with school administrators. In the 1930s and 1940s evaluation focused on learning-based behavioral changes, which were not closely associated with school administrators either. Only since the late 1950s have decisions become the focus of evaluation models (e.g., Cronbach, 1963; Stufflebeam, 1974; Scriven, 1973; Guba & Lincoln, 1981; Eisner, 1985). This has quite a bit to do with school administrators.

Indeed, in the past few decades evaluation as an administrative function and as practiced by evaluation professionals has expanded to include a variety of evaluation objects and evaluation methodologies. Three primary sets of objects of evaluation have emerged: student learning, teacher performance, and educational programs. Evaluation of student learning has included the domains of academic achievement, student aptitudes, student social behaviors, and student thought processes (e.g., Blum & Butler, 1985; Wittrock, 1986). In evaluation of teacher performance, focus has been on teacher effectiveness, competence, and performance (e.g., Darling-Hammond, Wise, & Pease, 1983). Another approach has included teaching methods, relationships with students, student evaluation procedures, and classroom management as the objects of teacher evaluation (DeRoche, 1987). A third set of foci of teacher evaluation has included instructional processes, interpersonal relationships, and professional responsibilities (e.g., Valentine, 1992).

The evaluation of educational programs has become a broad area, indeed. It has included program rationale, content, textbooks, role of teachers, budgeting, time, facilities, and effectiveness (DeRoche, 1987). Some of these evaluations have focused on a specific subject matter or grade level, such as reading (e.g., Guthrie, 1987), science and mathematics (e.g., Shavelson, McDonnell, & Oaks, 1989), and sixth-grade programs (e.g., Calfee, 1988).

Professional evaluators have improved their evaluation methodologies over the years (e.g., Berk, 1981). They have also expanded the variety of their methods to suit the purpose and object of the evaluation (e.g., Millman & Darling-Hammond, 1990; Popham, 1974; Glasman & Heck, 1992-1993).

Can school principals improve the quality of their evaluations by adopting the approaches and methods used by professional evaluators? The answer is probably "only somewhat." After all, the professional approaches and methods take much time to execute and principals do not have too much free time. The methods also incur costs that may not be covered by the schools even if principals conducted these evaluations themselves (analysis, etc.). Finally, principals do not have the technical competency that professional evaluators do in designing and executing evaluations.

Summary

In real life the evaluation that school administrators practice is rooted in specific problems that are administrative in nature and that derive from more general problematic situations in the school. For example, fighting among individual students involves a specific discipline problem and a specific safety problem. These problems are administrative in nature because the school principal has ultimate responsibility for how these problems are faced, treated, and solved. These problems derive from a broader problematic situation such as repeated gang violence or a temporary physical exchange of hot tempers. Real-life evaluation by an administrator begins when a problematic situation arises and the awareness of the specific problem(s) emerges.

This chapter highlighted principals' responses to externally mandated evaluations and to problem-driven, internally initiated evaluations. The chapter has also shown the ingredients of problem-rooted professional and systematic evaluations. Systematization was defined as singling out evaluation models, objects, and methodologies.

The next chapter builds on both of these kinds of evaluation. It employs the literature of educational administration to arrive at a structure of decision making. It uses also the literature on educational evaluation to derive a structure of evaluation. It then develops a joint structure of evaluation and decision making that resembles what actually occurs in administrative problem solving in schools.

2

PROBLEM-BASED
AND PROBLEM-DRIVEN
DECISIONS AND EVALUATIONS

Introduction

The study of school administration is in most part the study of administrative behaviors that are problem based and problem driven. It views administration as characterized in large part by problem-related choices that the principals make. Principals may deal with issues (e.g., Hoy & Miskel, 1991) such as disruptive or withdrawn students or rebellious or apathetic teachers. But these are usually symptoms of deeper pedagogical problems. Principals deal with the problems themselves. Attempts to improve learning (e.g., Drake & Roe, 1986; Ubben & Hughes, 1987) are one example. Some of these attempts may be organizational in nature. Others may deal with grouping of learners. Still others may focus on matching personnel with students or on the curriculum.

The principalship is filled with nonpedagogical, nonorganizational problems as well. Political problems exist, for example, when principals deal with insiders or outsiders to the school. Teachers may have different and hidden agendas. District office personnel

may "sweep." Community representatives may complain and sometimes blood let (e.g., Parkay & Hall, 1992, pp. 110-111). Conflict-related
problems may also exist (e.g., Lipham & Hoeh, 1974, pp. 132-148).
Principals may face interrole conflicts from simultaneously fulfilling two or more incompatible roles ("wearing many hats"). Principals may also have to work with many groups, each of them likely
to hold conflicting expectations for the principal role. They may also
face role-personality conflicts, or discrepancies between the basic
need-dispositions of the principal as an individual and the demands
placed on him or her as principal.

This chapter presents a problem-based and problem-driven model
of decisions and evaluations pertinent to school administrations
and then demonstrates the uses of the model. In one case, an administrator is faced with a problematic situation in which the identity of
the problems is unclear and their delineation incomplete. In the
other case, the problem is relatively clear and well delineated. Each
case includes key related decisions and corresponding evaluations.
The chapter also offers a data gathering and analysis instrument
that was developed from the model and presents as an example the
responses to the instrument recorded by one school principal.
These responses show that the problem-based principalship and the
problem-based model match.

The Model

The problem-based model consists of a problematic situation,
some key decisions that need to be made, and several corresponding
key evaluations. A problematic situation is included because administrators confront them regularly. They explain them in a consistent
way over time. Decisions and evaluations are included because together they constitute a style of analysis. Such an analysis untangles
the problematic situation and mitigates against acting too hurriedly.

Principals may be engaged in four key decisions during the
problem-based administrative process. Each decision initiates a
phase in this process. The phases include the problematic situation
phase, the problem phase, the solution phase, and the solution
implementation monitoring phase. At the beginning, principals are

faced with a problematic situation in which there are problems whose identity is unclear and whose delineation is incomplete. Principals have to make a decision: They choose whether or not to observe and participate in the problematic situation. If they decide to do so, then they are ready for the next three phases. They then need to choose the problem, select and implement a solution, and design a method for monitoring the solution implementation that they employ during the solution process.

The inclusion of key decisions in a problem-based administrative process was already conceived in the 1950s. Griffith (1958), for example, asserted that administrative decisions are the substance of the administrator's work. A decision, according to Griffith, implied judgment that affected the course of action. The point of decision was a solution to a preferred course of action.

Simon (1961) looked in depth at the administrator's decisions within the context of the organization. He specified the administrator's function as allocating authority to the role and as setting limits to the decisions. Simon proposed that decision behaviors are purposive and that they involve conscious or unconscious selection of particular actions. More recently, Hanson (1991) offered a view of decisions as points within the problem-solving process. He examined the decisions as choice opportunities whereby the organization is expected to produce problem-solving decisions. According to Hanson, the choice opportunities are affected by institutionalized routine, external factors, and social processes. Leithwood and Montgomery (1986) also viewed continuously made individual decisions as key elements of a comprehensive problem-solving process.

An administrator's decision to observe and participate in a problematic situation is rooted in the problematic situation itself. Hemphill (1958) called the situation a dissatisfying state of affairs. He differentiated between problem situations that involve the characteristics of the nonperson environment and those that involve the characteristics of the personal environment. Hemphill saw the former as the individual's problem and the latter as a social problem involving face-to-face interactions within groups of individuals. Hoy and Miskel (1991) called the problematic situation the context within which symptoms are found. They chose as their first step in the problem-solving process the identification of symptoms and

proposed that the symptoms themselves may be identified by preliminary information that suggests a problem. The information
contained in the 30 cases described in this book (10 in Chapter 3 and
the other 20 in Resource A) actually relates to problems in schools
and their milieus. When Hoy and Miskel write about finding symptoms of problems they imply the hope that problems themselves
will also be found.

The second decision in this model is to choose one or more problems to work on. Hanson (1991) suggests that there is a constant stream
of problems and a fluid participation of participants who choose to
engage or not, as a function of the time and energy that they can
devote to it. Both Hoy and Miskel (1991) and Lunenberg and Ornstein (1991) propose that the identification of the problem is the first
prerequisite in this stage. Hoy and Miskel define the problem as the
difference between expected and actual outcomes. Lunenberg and
Ornstein define it as a discrepancy between existing and desired
conditions.

Determining the extent of a discrepancy may be done by measuring results, comparing them to objectives, determining the significance of the difference, and communicating threshold differences.
Lunenberg and Ornstein (1991, pp. 161-162) suggest specific activities in the identification of the problems and in assuming responsibility for working on those that were chosen. According to them,
there is a need to recognize the problem, determine a standard level
of performance, divide complex problematic situations into specific
problems, and, finally, set priorities. The authors recommend that
the problem specification be done in terms of what, where, when,
and how.

In relation to the third decision—to choose a solution and implement it—Leithwood and Montgomery (1986) emphasize the choice
notion here because they believe that there may be many possible
solutions and that each problem should have a chosen solution.
Hanson (1991) also believes in the flow of solutions and in the need
to choose. Lunenberg and Ornstein (1991) argue that sharing information and analyzing it expedites the choice of a solution. They also
believe in generating several possible alternative solutions. Hoy
and Miskel (1991) detail the activities associated with choosing a
solution. They include the description of organizational elements and

environmental elements. They also include assessing the congru-
ence between the two sets of information, diagnosing the problem's
causes, and formulating a plan.

The fourth and last decision is to choose a design for monitoring
solution implementation and to implement this design. In many
ways this decision constitutes the choice of an evaluation plan (Hoy
& Miskel, 1991). It involves a preliminary specification of criteria
that serve to monitor the solution implementation (Stufflebeam,
1971)—summative criteria in the language of professional evaluation (Scriven, 1967). Clearly, this decision is related to the outcome
of the previous three decisions. It is not, however, an interpretation
of results emanating from previous decisions. Rather, it is a proactive phase (Gally, 1982) just as the other three phases were.

In addition to a problematic situation and four key decisions, the
model is composed of evaluative activities. A selected number of
evaluation objects pertaining to the decision to observe and participate in the problematic situation are listed below:

1. The problematic issues (What are they?)
2. The origins of the issues (What are they?)
3. The participants in the issues (Who are they? How are they
   participating?)
4. Those responsible for the issues (Who are they? How are they
   responsible?)
5. The possible specific problems (What are they?)
6. The owners of the problems (Who are they? How are they
   owners?)
7. The priorities of the problem owners (What are they?)
8. The possible effects of each problem, if it continues to exist
   (What are they?)
9. The predicted manageability of each problem, if it continues
   to exist (What is it?)

A selected list of evaluation objects pertaining to the decision to
choose one or more problems to work on is presented below:

1. The alternative solutions (What are they?)

2. The potential owners of each solution (Who are they? How are they owners?)
3. The priorities of the solution owners (What are they?)
4. The possible effects of each solution (What are they?)
5. The cost of each solution (What is it?)
6. The manageability of each solution (What is it?)

The next decision in the problem-based administrative process is to choose a solution and implement it. Related evaluation objects include:

1. The implementation process (What is it?)
2. The effectiveness of the process (What is it?)
3. The manageability of the process (What is it?)
4. The cost of the process (What is it?)
5. The owners of the process (Who are they? How are they owners?)

The final major decision in the administrative process is choosing a design for monitoring solution implementation and implementing this design. Corresponding evaluation objects include:

1. The cost of the monitoring of the solution implementation (What is it?)
2. The potential effectiveness of the monitoring solution implementation (What is it?)

The evaluation objects suggested above as part of the problem-based and problem-driven administrative process include issues, participants, problem owners, priorities, cost, manageability, and potential effectiveness. Most of these evaluative items are descriptive. Some are also judgmental. Most of the questions deal with "school process" descriptors much more than they do with "school product" ones. They do not include questions such as "Are the expected effects achieved?" or "Is the program producing?" or "What are the most efficient programs?" (House, 1980, p. 23). Also not included are evaluation questions such as "How good is the performance?" or

"Does the program meet its goals?" or "What are the program's actual failures?" (Patton, 1978, pp. 152-155).

When school administrators ask themselves about evaluation objects, they actually reflect on what Stewart (1982) and Sergiovanni (1987) call demands, constraints, and choices associated with the problem-based job. Demands are those aspects of the job that cannot be avoided. Constraints are those aspects that limit what an administrator can do. Choices are represented by the opportunities to be different from others in similar circumstances.

Each time school administrators ask about an evaluation object they start a minievaluation process that consists of two additional questions. One is about the evaluation methodology they use to collect data and judge the evaluation object. The other is about the evaluation findings.

In relation to each of the objects of evaluation there is one or more evaluation methodologies. To put it differently, what is to be evaluated determines how it should be evaluated. More than one method is needed to evaluate any one of the evaluation objects because the objects themselves are complex and, to a large extent, unknown. For example, the first of the four key decisions is followed by nine corresponding objects to be evaluated. The first object, the problematic issues, may be ascertained through observation and listening. The second object, the origins of the issues, may be assessed by reading documents and interviewing. Observation and listening may apply to the third object, participants. Constructing associative relationships among data on other items may apply to the fourth object, those responsible for the problems.

The evaluation of the other five objects requires quite a bit more judgment than the evaluation of the first four. This is true for sorting problems, identifying their owners, listing the owners' priorities, predicting possible effects of the problem, and assessing the predicted manageability of the problems. The same is true for the listed objects to be evaluated that follow any one of the other three decisions. Judgment has to be rendered about data collected in relation to solution-related objects, solution implementation-related objects, and solution implementation monitoring-related objects. Considerably less judgment is rendered early in the problem-based administrative evaluation process than in later stages. Problem-based and problem-driven administrative realities dictate this situation.

An Illustrative Case
of a Problematic Situation

The case (Kowalski, 1991, Case #5, pp. 40-46) is that of a high school principal, Allen Miller, who devotes most of his workday to meeting with students, teachers, and parents, and his assistant principal, who is the "enforcer" in the school but who wears wrinkled clothes. Mr. Miller has given his assistant principal several positive evaluations but is now told by the superintendent and associate superintendent that the assistant principal's appearance has become intolerable and that he will have to be transferred and "demoted" to a physical education teacher. Mr. Miller puts up an argument but is told that, instead, his support for the decision is needed and that he should keep silent while the move is made. It is emphasized to him that "it would be the superintendent's decision, not his."

The usefulness of the problem-based administrative evaluation model will now be examined in relation to Mr. Miller's dilemma. If he chooses to observe and participate in the problematic situation, he will have actually chosen to review and analyze what is going on and what *might* be going on.

Mr. Miller has been a principal in this high school for the past 9 years. He has already had a chance to get to know (for 4 years) the associate superintendent who runs the meetings with the principals. He is not as familiar with the superintendent, who has been in the district for only 2 years and who only infrequently conducts meetings with the principals. If Mr. Miller is to gather any more data, it might be obtained from some principals who would provide different perceptions and maybe also some new data. At the initial stages of the observation of the problematic situation, it may be unwise for Mr. Miller to "advertise" the issue by talking about it.

The model suggests nine evaluation objects that are evaluated after the decision to observe and participate in the problematic situation has taken place. The first object focuses on the problematic issues themselves. Following is a selection of some such issues:

1. To remove an effective assistant principal is a great loss.
2. The working style of the principal has been in large part a function of the working style of the assistant principal, who has been in the school longer.

3. It is unfair to the assistant principal that the superintendent and the associate superintendent introduce personal issues into his personnel evaluation case.

4. It is curious that images that the community has of district employees show up at the school-building level.

5. The nature of symbolic leadership in this high school is strange.

6. To assume that the superintendent and the associate superintendent represent the district to the community more than the principal and the assistant principal do is to consider district politics more important than school-building politics.

7. When the superintendent and the associate superintendent exercise evaluation authority over the principal's evaluation authority, they politicize evaluation in the district.

8. How the school board will vote on the superintendent's recommendation is not clear.

The second evaluation object includes the origin of the issues. There are probably at least two origins to these issues. One is the high socioeconomic image (upper middle class) of the community, the school system, the high school, and the high school principal. The other source includes feelings that parents of some high school students have about the personal appearance and other personal characteristics of the assistant principal.

Who participates in these issues is the third evaluation object. Participants possibly include:

1. The principal
2. The assistant principal
3. The superintendent
4. The associate superintendent
5. Some unhappy high school students
6. Perhaps other principals (silently)

The fourth evaluation object is who is responsible for the issues. Included here are the principal, superintendent, and associate superintendent.

Evaluation objects numbers five through nine (which follow that same first decision) deal with specific problems. Object five focuses on the problems themselves. There could be many problems, of course, such as:

1. The assistant principal brings a lawsuit against the district if the school board approves the superintendent's recommendations to transfer and demote him.
2. The school board may not unanimously accept the superintendent's recommendation.
3. The principal's authority suffers from the removal of the assistant principal and from the devaluing of his evaluation of the assistant principal.
4. The principal agrees to be silent against his best judgment (ethical problem).
5. The principal changes his mind and agrees with the move (consistency problem).
6. The principal disagrees with the move and voices his opinion about it (defiance problem).

Evaluation object six deals with the owners of the problems. Respectively, the school board owns the first, the superintendent owns the second, and the principal owns the other four problems. The last problem is also owned jointly by the superintendent and associate superintendent.

The final three evaluation objects (seven through nine) that follow the first decision focus respectively on priorities of problem owners, effects of problems, and manageability of problems. Table 2.1 summarizes these evaluation objects. Evaluation objects that follow, respectively, the second, third, and fourth key decisions are described in the next section.

An Illustrative Case of a Known Problem

Getzels (1979) distinguished between three kinds of problem situations. The first is the "presented" problem situation in which the problem exists. It has a known formulation, a known method of solution, and a known solution. The second kind is the "discovered" problem situation. Here, the problem also exists but it may or may not have a known formulation, a known method of solution, or a

TABLE 2.1 Priorities of Problem Owners, Effects of Problems, and Manageability of Problems as Evaluation Objects

Problem	Problem Owner's Priorities	Possible Effects of Problem if It Continues to Exist	Predicted Manageability of Problem
The lawsuit possibility	High priority to keep the board and district free of conflict	Loss in court for the district, loss of revenues, media involvement in district affairs, loss of good image	Board could be placed in a situation where it acts according to another agency's directives
The split board possibility	High priority implement what the board votes on	Loss of job for the superintendent	For the superintendent, manageability will remain a function of support from the board and others in the district
The possibility of weakening the principal's authority	High priority to be able to adjust in the management of the school	Loss of help for the principal, need to change work style, need for ensurance of authority for rehiring	Principal could lose discretionary powers
The possibility of the principal's agreement to remain silent	High priority to handle ethical problems	Loss of respect for the principal	Principal could lose ability to withstand pressure

18

| The possibility of the principal's change of mind to support the district office | High priority to handle consistency problems | Loss of teachers' confidence in the principal | Principal could lose ability to lead |
| The possibility of the principal voicing his opposition | High priority to handle pressure from the district leadership | Loss of job for the principal | Principal could lose ability to remain in district |

known solution. The third kind of a problem situation is a "created" one in which the problem does not exist until someone creates it (Getzels, 1979, pp. 7-8).[1]

In the previous section, the focus was on the problematic situation in which the problem had to be discovered or created—discovered in cases where information attested to its existence and created when there was no such information. Typically, empirical work (Getzels, 1979) or "policy" analysis work (Boyd & Immegard, 1979) has to be done when one moves from a created situation to a discovered situation. Discovered problems in the principalship usually include the need to raise student achievement test scores (Glasman, 1986a) or the need to modify the curriculum (Lunenberg & Ornstein, 1991, chap. 13). These needs occur, respectively, when the scores are too low and should be higher or when the curriculum needs revision. Created problems in the principalship usually occur when observation and analysis bring them about.

An example of the use of the rest of the problem-based administrative model is the case of the high school principal who is now faced with a specific and known problem. Assume that the problem he decides to work on is to convince the superintendent and the associate superintendent to defer for one year their decision to recommend to the school board the transfer and demotion of the assistant high school principal. The principal will plan to work with the assistant principal during this time, helping him to fit the image of the school and the school system. If they are successful, then the recommendation to the board will not be forthcoming. If they are not successful, then the recommendation will be made. Assume also that the major reason why the principal chooses to work on this problem is his desire to avoid the transfer and demotion of his assistant and at the same time to eliminate complaints about him.

The decision to work on this problem generates six evaluation objects, according to the problem-based administrative model. The evaluation objects that might be pertinent to the case of the high school principal's chosen problem are:

1. The alternative solutions: Contact the superintendent alone, the associate superintendent alone, or both, and make the case to them.

2. The potential owners of each solution: in the first case, the superintendent and the principal; in the second case, the associate superintendent and the principal; and in the third case, all three of them.

3. The priorities of the solution owners: for the superintendent to eliminate complaints about the assistant principal; for the associate superintendent to abide by the superintendent's wishes and to remain in control of the principal; and for the principal not to lose the assistant principal.

4. The possible effects of each solution: probably identical.

5. The cost of each solution: If the superintendent is contacted directly, the cost of not going through the associated superintendent may be high, in the long run; if the associated superintendent is contacted, the cost of not going directly to the superintendent may be reasonably high if the associate superintendent is against the idea; if the superintendent and associated superintendent are approached together, the cost of being turned down may be very high.

6. The manageability of each solution: probably identical.

The model's next decision point is for the principal to choose and implement a solution. Suppose that his choice is to contact the superintendent and associate superintendent together in order to make the case for deferring making a recommendation to the board. The problem-based administrative process model includes five corresponding evaluation objects. These are listed along with specific ones pertinent to the case:

1. The implementation process: a carefully crafted set of arguments focusing on (a) the superb performance of the assistant principal; (b) his ability to continue to grow and change if stimulated to do so; (c) the justification of the complaints against him; (d) the injustice of making drastic changes in the assistant principal's work conditions without giving him a chance to improve; (e) the support system that the assistant principal has accumulated over 24 years in the district; (f) the need to convey all of the above to those who had complained against the assistant principal; (g) the request of support for the principal in his desire to keep the assistant principal; (h) the difficulties the principal might experience in remaining

silent due to ethical questions, especially if the recommendation is made to the board; and (i) the offer to do anything else
that might further the chance of having the superintendent
accept the principal's request.

2. The effectiveness of the process: high because all three potential owners of the solution are present, there is ample time
before the superintendent must take action, and it is still possible to contact complainers with new information and possible
alternative solutions.

3. The manageability of the process: under control.

4. The cost of the process: There are time slots, possible breach
of confidentiality costs, and costs of failure to convince the
superintendent.

5. The owners of the process: The principal, the associate superintendent, and the superintendent are owners by virtue of
their involvement in the process.

The model's final decision point is for the principal to choose a
design for monitoring solution implementation and to implement
the design. Suppose that the principal did not hear anything new
from either the superintendent or the associate superintendent after
he made his argument to them. All he heard was repetitions of the
comments from the last time they met, such as ". . . this is a special
community. . . . [This is] a special high school. . . . We have become
increasingly concerned about the image our administrators present
to the general public. . . . Visitors to the school could easily mistake
him [the assistant principal] for a custodian." ". . . he has to go . . . he
won't be angry with you . . . he'll direct his outrage at [us]. . . ." ". . .
we have given it a great deal of thought . . . we want your assurance
that you will go along. . . ." (Kowalski, 1991, pp. 44-45).

The principal is lucky to be heard again, even though they seem
to have made up their mind. He is bothered, however, that he hears
no reactions to his statement, just silence. On this basis, he may
make a specific choice regarding the monitoring solution implementation design. Suppose that he chooses to monitor by asking
questions about his own previous statement. Examples might include, "Did you hear this or that point?" "Are you disputing this or
that point?"

The problem-based administrative model offers two evaluation objects corresponding to the last major decision. Following are these two objects along with examples of objects pertinent to this case:

1. The cost of the monitoring solution implementation design: high cost because of the need to repeat items and prompt listeners to react to them when apparently they do not wish to. The cost includes time, possible alienation, possible anger causing, and the appearance of being stubborn.

2. The potential effectiveness of the monitoring solution implementation design: effective only if it produces acceptance of argument or reveals previously unknown information such as hidden agendas, including political objectives or objectives related to the principal himself.

A Data Gathering and Analysis Instrument

The instrument described here was developed from the problem-based and driven administrative model outlined earlier. As you can see, the complete instrument consists of an introductory page as well as four additional parts. Each of these parts is associated with one major decision made by the principal throughout the problem-solving process. Following each decision are 22 sets of evaluations. Each set of evaluations includes the evaluation object, methodologies, and findings. The complete instrument is shown in Figure 2.1.

A Test of the Instrument

A test of the instrument took place in June of 1991. Participants in a week-long workshop on education administration held in Los Angeles were asked to choose a problematic situation that they had recently experienced. They were asked to describe the situation and then to attempt to record the four decisions and the 22 sets of evaluation that were pertinent to the case. The purpose of this test was to ascertain how relevant the items in the instrument were to the problematic situations the principals chose and how easily they could recall these items. The principals filled in the items in their leisure

(*text continues on page 29*)

Figure 2.1. Evaluation Instrument (pages 24-28)

BACKGROUND INFORMATION: Grade levels in school _____ Number of students in school _____

Years you have been in the present job _____ Number of administrators in the school _____

DESCRIBE A PROBLEMATIC SITUATION YOU FACED RECENTLY: _____

_____

_____

_____

_____

_____

_____

_____

_____

_____

_____

_____

_____

_____

_____

_____

_____

_____

_____

_____

A. DID YOU DECIDE TO OBSERVE AND PARTICIPATE IN THE PROBLEMATIC SITUATION?

WHAT DID YOU LOOK FOR?	HOW DID YOU LOOK AT IT?	WHAT DID YOU FIND?
THE PROBLEMATIC ISSUES		
THE ORIGIN OF THE ISSUES		
THE PARTICIPANTS IN THE ISSUES		
THOSE RESPONSIBLE FOR THE ISSUES		
POSSIBLE SPECIFIC PROBLEMS TO WORK ON		
THE OWNERS OF POSSIBLE PROBLEMS		
THE PRIORITIES OF PROBLEM OWNERS		
THE POSSIBLE EFFECTS OF THE PROBLEMS		
THE PREDICTED MANAGEABILITY OF THE PROBLEMS		

(continued)

25

B. DID YOU DECIDE ON A PROBLEM TO WORK ON? IF SO, WHAT WAS THE PROBLEM? _____

WHAT DID YOU LOOK FOR?	HOW DID YOU LOOK AT IT?	WHAT DID YOU FIND OUT?
THE POSSIBLE SOLUTIONS OF THE PROBLEM CHOSEN TO WORK ON		
THE OWNERS OF THE POSSIBLE SOLUTIONS		
THE PRIORITIES OF SOLUTION OWNERS		
THE POSSIBLE EFFECTS OF THE SOLUTIONS		
THE COST OF THE SOLUTIONS		
THE MANAGEABILITY OF THE SOLUTIONS		

C. DID YOU DECIDE ON A SOLUTION AND DID YOU IMPLEMENT IT? IF SO, WHAT WAS THE SOLUTION?

WHAT DID YOU LOOK FOR?	HOW DID YOU LOOK AT IT?	WHAT DID YOU FIND OUT?
THE SOLUTION IMPLEMENTATION PROCESS		
THE POSSIBLE EFFECTIVENESS OF THE SOLUTION IMPLEMENTATION PROCESS		
THE PREDICTED MANAGEABILITY OF THE SOLUTION IMPLEMENTATION PROCESS		
THE COST OF THE SOLUTION IMPLEMENTATION PROCESS		
THE OWNERS OF THE SOLUTION IMPLEMENTATION PROCESS		

(continued)

27

D. DID YOU DECIDE ON A DESIGN FOR A MONITORING SOLUTION IMPLEMENTATION AND DID YOU
   IMPLEMENT IT? IF SO, WHAT WAS THE DESIGN? _____

WHAT DID YOU LOOK FOR?	HOW LONG DID YOU LOOK AT IT?	WHAT DID YOU FIND OUT?
THE COST OF THE DESIGN FOR A MONITORING SOLUTION IMPLEMENTATION		
THE POSSIBLE EFFECTIVENESS OF THE DESIGN FOR A MONITORING SOLUTION IMPLEMENTATION		

time and they reported that it had taken them from 75 to 105 minutes to respond.

The results were as follows: Eight principals responded; two could not. The chosen problematic situations among those who responded included examples from the areas of personnel administration, pupil personnel administration, and curriculum development. Two of the eight principals were able to provide all the needed responses and six were able to provide about 80% of the responses. No clarification was provided by the author regarding any of the items.

The instrument was further tested by interviewing principals rather than having them fill in the responses in writing. The objective was to see if the response rate increased when the interviewer clarified items when necessary. Five other participants in a similar workshop in June of 1992 were interviewed in Los Angeles. All five were able to provide all needed answers. One participant was a principal who had administered a private school for 19 years. A condensed and edited version of her full response appears in Figure 2.2.

Summary

This chapter has presented a problem-based administrative model and illustrative cases that served to demonstrate the usefulness of the model. The overall model should be clear by now. The first step relates to situations where the actual problem is not yet known. The central decision that needs to be made is to choose to observe and participate in the problematic situation in order to be able to sort out the problems. The second step involves situations where the problems are or become known. There are three decisions here: to choose a problem to work on, to choose a solution and implement it, and to choose a monitoring solution implementation design and implement it.

Each of these decisions generates objects that need to be evaluated. Nine such evaluation objects follow the first decision, six follow the second, five follow the third, and two follow the fourth.

A difficult case was chosen to demonstrate the usefulness of the model. A high school administrator is called in by the superintendent and associate superintendent and is surprised to hear criticism about his assistant and about his evaluation of the assistant's performance.

(*text continues on page 36*)

Figure 2.2. Evaluation Instrument: A Test (pages 30-35)

BACKGROUND INFORMATION: Grade levels in school K-10 Number of students in school ___250___

Years you have been in the present job ___19 (22)___ Number of administrators in the school ___1___

DESCRIBE A PROBLEMATIC SITUATION YOU FACED RECENTLY:

The situation involves a very weak Hebrew teacher who also had personal problems at home. Complaints about her conduct in class increased. She appeared not to be in control of her emotions. She yelled frequently. She did not hand in lesson plans and attendance sheets. There was growing evidence that she came to class unprepared. Students were falling behind in their Hebrew skills. During the middle of the year, she ended up being in the process of divorcing her spouse. Soon afterwards she entered the hospital for a month. The principal and the rabbi determined not to dismiss her even though her performance after the hospital stay remained extremely weak.

A. DID YOU DECIDE TO OBSERVE AND PARTICIPATE IN THE PROBLEMATIC SITUATION? Yes

WHAT DID YOU LOOK FOR?	HOW DID YOU LOOK AT IT?	WHAT DID YOU FIND OUT?
THE PROBLEMATIC ISSUES	Class visitation Class visitation, talking to students and parents Class visitation Discussion with parents	Students' growing deficiency in Hebrew Students' growing unhappiness in class Teacher's worsening performance Parents' growing dissatisfaction
THE ORIGIN OF THE ISSUES	Working with teacher for a while Working with teacher for a while	Inherent weakness of the teacher Retaining the teacher
THE PARTICIPANTS IN THE ISSUES	Discussions with rabbi Observing the teacher Observing the students in class Discussions with parents	Principal and rabbi Teacher Students in teacher's class Parents of students
THOSE RESPONSIBLE FOR THE ISSUES	Considers on her own Discussions with rabbi Discussions with teacher	Principal Rabbi Teacher
POSSIBLE SPECIFIC PROBLEMS TO WORK ON	Discussions with rabbi Discussions with teachers Considers on her own	Overall school's credibility Teaching staff's morale Principal's credibility and professional ability
THE OWNERS OF POSSIBLE PROBLEMS	Observing the rabbi Considers on her own Considers on her own Considers on her own	Principal and rabbi Teacher and other teaching staff members Students Parents

(continued)

31

THE PRIORITIES OF PROBLEM OWNERS	Considers on her own Discussions with teacher Discussions with students Discussions with teachers	Principal: appropriate learning/ teaching/leadership Teacher: health, salary, learning Students: learning, accepted by teacher, safety Teaching staff: professional and good social environment
THE POSSIBLE EFFECTS OF THE PROBLEMS	Considers on her own Considers on her own Considers on her own Considers on her own	Student unhappiness Parents leave school Teachers upset with lack of professional leadership Principal's lack of credibility
THE PREDICTED MANAGEABILITY OF THE PROBLEMS	Discussions with parents Discussions with teachers Writing to parents	Students with average ability can receive tutor's help Need teachers' trust in leadership Need to inform parents about intervention

B. DID YOU DECIDE ON A PROBLEM TO WORK ON? Yes. IF SO, WHAT WAS THE PROBLEM?   How 1 effect of the teacher's performance and illness on student learning.

WHAT DID YOU LOOK FOR?	HOW DID YOU LOOK AT IT?	WHAT DID YOU FI
THE POSSIBLE SOLUTIONS OF THE PROBLEM CHOSEN TO WORK ON	Discussions with teacher, rabbi Discussions with teacher Discussions with rabbi	Place coteacher in class Use pullout tutoring Dismiss teacher
THE OWNERS OF THE POSSIBLE SOLUTIONS	Considers on her own Discussions with the rabbi Considers on her own Considers on her own	Teacher Principal and rabbi Coteacher or replacemen Students
THE PRIORITIES OF SOLUTION OWNERS	Considers on her own Discussions with rabbi Discussions with rabbi Considers on her own	Teacher: maintain positio Principal: stabilize situati Rabbi: stabilize situation Students: time spent usef
THE POSSIBLE EFFECTS OF THE SOLUTIONS	Considers on her own Considers on her own Considers on her own	Coteacher: additional cos Pullout tutor: additional Dismiss teacher: principa credibility as caring
THE COST OF THE SOLUTIONS	Considers on her own	First two solutions: subst
THE MANAGEABILITY OF THE SOLUTIONS	Considers on her own Discussions with teachers Considers on her own	Morally wrong to dismiss Coteacher: a problem Pullout tutoring: manage

C. DID YOU DECIDE ON A SOLUTION AND DID YOU IMPLEMENT IT? Yes. IF SO, WHAT WAS THE SOLUTION?
Hire a second tutor.

WHAT DID YOU LOOK FOR?	HOW DID YOU LOOK AT IT?	WHAT DID YOU FIND OUT?
THE SOLUTION IMPLEMENTATION PROCESS	Discussion with teacher Considers on her own Discussion with teacher	Select a tutor and students, determine tutorial time Elicit parent support Meet regularly with teacher and visit her classroom
THE POSSIBLE EFFECTIVENESS OF THE SOLUTION IMPLEMENTATION PROCESS	Observing students Observing teacher	Students progressing slowly Teacher brings lesson plans to meeting principal
THE PREDICTED MANAGEABILITY OF THE SOLUTION IMPLEMENTATION PROCESS	Considers on her own Considers on her own Observing class	Time-consuming Difficult to work with teacher in an intensive follow-up Pullout is somewhat disruptive
THE COST OF THE SOLUTION IMPLEMENTATION PROCESS	Considers on her own	Tutor salary
THE OWNERS OF THE SOLUTION IMPLEMENTATION PROCESS	Considers on her own Discussions with teacher Discussions with tutor Considers on her own	Principal Teacher Tutor Students

D. DID YOU DECIDE ON A DESIGN FOR A MONITORING SOLUTION IMPLEMENTATION AND DID YOU IMPLEMENT IT? Yes. IF SO, WHAT WAS THE DESIGN? Discussions with teacher, tutor, and parents.

WHAT DID YOU LOOK FOR?	HOW LONG DID YOU LOOK AT IT?	WHAT DID YOU FIND OUT?
THE COST OF THE DESIGN FOR A MONITORING SOLUTION IMPLEMENTATION	Considers on her own	Principal's time was significant
THE POSSIBLE EFFECTIVENESS OF THE DESIGN FOR A MONITORING SOLUTION IMPLEMENTATION	Observing students, discussions with them Considers on her own Discussions with parents Considers on her own, discussions with tutor	Students progressing but still unhappy Teacher was dismissed at the end of the year Parents were supportive Average student in the fall of the following year received tutorial help

35

His support is solicited in ousting the assistant even though his own work and the assistant's have been complementary to each other. The principal is not consulted at any time. His support for the decision is solicited.

The choice of a difficult administrative case for this chapter was deliberate. The intention was primarily to show that the emphasis on and the choice of evaluation objects is possible and useful even in such cases. The usefulness of evaluation objects that correspond to specific decisions showed in the preparation of an argument against demotion and transfer of an assistant principal. The value of the evaluation objects proposed in this model would remain whether each of the four decisions is made separately, chronologically and at different times, or when principals work simultaneously on more than one problem.

Evaluation as practiced by school administrators is rooted in the existence of problematic situations and specific problems that are administrative in nature. Chapter 1 highlighted problem-driven principals' responses to externally mandated evaluation. It also described problem-driven internally initiated evaluations. Even politicized evaluations are rooted in the existence of problems.

The systematic evaluations described in Chapter 1 are also rooted in problems, but these are evaluators' problems. The history of systematic evaluation suggests, for example, that when student learning constituted the evaluative problem, systematized evaluation improved its testing and measurement procedures. As curricula foci became objects of evaluation, new objective-based evaluation methods developed. When work had to center on teacher evaluation, new appropriate evaluative approaches such as portfolios, self-assessment, and observations had to be developed.

It turns out, then, that all evaluations are rooted in problematic situations. Evaluation as practiced by school administrators is grounded in administrative problematic situations; systematic evaluation as practiced by evaluators is grounded in evaluative problematic situations. The model that this chapter has provided features administrative processes that are driven by problematic situations and that include four decisions and 22 evaluations.

The instrument described in this chapter provided interesting information about a principal's decisions and evaluations while facing the problematic situation involving the weak teacher. The principal's humanistic and rational concomitant approaches seemed to be consistent throughout the process. At any given time it was possible to detect both orientations in action.

The data lend confidence to the usefulness of the instrument itself. According to the responses, the principal was able to sort out the various evaluations without much difficulty. She had engaged in all 22 evaluations and within each one she had dealt with all of the three critical questions. She identified each object ("What did you look at?"), each methodology ("How did you look at it?"), and each conclusion ("What did you find?"). Of particular note were the consistencies between earlier and later conclusions as well as between methodologies and corresponding conclusions.

In discussions with all 15 respondents several additional phenomena became clear. Clarification of items in an interview format may produce 100% or close to 100% responses from everyone. The issues that need clarification are language issues. Also, it is essential to ask principals for a very recent problematic situation or for one with which they spent quite a bit of time. Principals appear to be remember both situations relatively well.

Most of the evaluation methodologies pertain to both data gathering and rendering judgment about the data. The exception of the methodology of "considers on her own" usually involves judgment rendering on data integration, not data collection. Whereas this alone is probably insufficient to justify a change in the definition of evaluation, it nonetheless provides a case for redefining at a later date the components of an evaluation administrative function. Also, in all 15 sets of responses there were cases of more than one evaluation conclusion emanating from one evaluation methodology and of more than one evaluation methodology leading to no more than one evaluation conclusion. The evaluation methodology-conclusion link in administration may not necessarily be identical to its counterpart in systematic evaluation.

The instrument itself seems to fit the reality of what principals think and do under problematic conditions. It appears to be a highly valid way of describing how they evaluate and decide. The work of the principal is certainly not always linear (see problems → seek solutions → implement them → monitor them). The applicability of the instrument described here is, therefore, more limited in such conditions.

Note

1. I wish to thank an anonymous reviewer for having remarked to me that Getzels later dropped his "created problem" from his typology for administrators.

3

CASES OF ADMINISTRATIVE
USE OF EVALUATION

The Conducting of Administrative
Evaluations by Elementary School Principals

This chapter contains brief accounts of 10 interviews conducted with school administrators with the aid of the interview protocol described in Chapter 2. Thirty interviews were conducted in all; the other 20 are summarized in Resource A. Due to the minutiae of detail that the administrators provided in the interviews, the accounts here summarize only portions of their responses to the protocol questions. At the principals' own request, any identifying details have been disguised or omitted to ensure confidentiality. The promise of confidentiality had the added benefit of allowing the principals to speak freely and be exceedingly frank. The responses themselves were to the question to describe the problematic situation, the four questions about decisions made, and the 22 sets of questions about the use of evaluation.

The 30 principals were located in seven Southern California cities in Orange, Los Angeles, Ventura, and Santa Barbara counties. The cases took place in 27 different schools. Of the 30 administrators, 10 were female (2 of whom were also minorities), and 9 were minorities

(2 of whom were also female). In most cases the interviews took place in the administrator's office; a few took place in the writer's office. The interviews lasted between 40 and 60 minutes.

CASE #1

When Parents Do Not Want
Their Children in a Bilingual Class

This principal, Mr. José Arriaga, has administered the same school for 10 years. The school enrolls 600 students, over 60% of whom are of minority background. The principal noticed that the percentage of limited-English-proficient (LEP) students was increasing rapidly. In the year that just ended, he had established 12 bilingual classes with 12 Spanish-speaking teachers. A very large proportion of the parents of English-only students preferred not to have their children enroll in these mixed bilingual classes. Were he not to set up the mixed classes, however, he would have been accused of promoting segregation. Legally, he could not force English-only students into bilingual classes. But if he did not push for such classes, he would have ended up with unbalanced class size: an average of 16 students in each bilingual class and 32 in each English-only class. The problem was pervasive in kindergarten, first grade, and second grade. From the third grade on, parents' preference focused more on teachers' strength than on the bilingual issue. Furthermore, the principal felt constrained by the teachers' union. The question he faced in May was: What to do in the upcoming school year? He faced instructional and school-community relations issues.

Mr. Arriaga decided to observe and participate in the problematic situation, as he had in each of the past years. He consulted pertinent documentation issued by the district's office. He was also one of several principals in the district who talked extensively about these issues both formally in meetings and informally on a one-to-one basis. This year the principal talked to many English-only parents about the subject and sensed that they were intensifying their resistance to bilingual classes. Although he needed to officially advise them that they had the right not to enroll or to withdraw their children from the bilingual class they were in, he did not send such a letter. He was afraid that too many of the parents would withdraw their children. Instead, he planned to set up classes without sending the letter, reasoning that if parents protested, he would permit transfers out. The principal saw the origin of these problematic issues to be the sharp increase in the student diversity in the school and the district.

Based on his many discussions on the topic, Mr. Arriaga saw all teachers in the school, parents of English-only students, and himself as participants in the issues. He considered himself alone as responsible. As he sorted out the problems, he saw three central ones. One was whether to continue not sending a letter to parents. A second one was what to do when a parent requested a transfer. The third concern was what to do when instructional problems occurred in the bilingual classes themselves. The principal considered himself the owner of these problems along with the district office's assistant superintendent. For both of these men, these problems overshadowed all other problems. If the problems lingered, students would be transferred out of the school and parents who were active in the PTA and in fund-raising would be lost to the school. Mr. Arriaga felt that he could manage the problems but that an increasing number of neighborhood residents would be displeased with the transfer of minority students into the school.

The principal decided to work on the following matter: create an awareness on the part of the English-only parents about tangible advantages for them if their children enrolled in the program. Based on discussions with other principals, he thought of offering lessons in how to speak Spanish using a variety of cultural-based approaches. He felt that he owned this possible solution, which he considered to be of a high priority with potential positive effects emanating from this approach. Costs would include child care and busing. He did not think that managing this program would be difficult.

Mr. Arriaga decided that he was going to convince the parents to enroll their children. Again, after consulting with other principals and also with his staff and the school site council he approached the English-only parents and asked them about their enrollment intent. He talked to them about the advantages of speaking Spanish. He expected some of the parents to accept the offer and some to take their children out of the school instead. He thought that he could manage the solution well. The cost would be 30 extra minutes of teaching Spanish daily, training of teachers, and purchasing curriculum material—not a prohibitive cost, compared to similar programs for children. The principal felt that both he and the teachers would own the solution implementation process. He decided on a monitoring solution implementation design. He would meet from time to time with teachers, students, and parents to find out how things were progressing. The cost of this monitoring was going to involve time on his part. He also expected that teachers would ask for release time. Mr. Arriaga believed that ultimately an evaluation of student achievement was going to be necessary.

CASE #2

When Teachers From the Same School
Compete for a Newly Opened Position in Their School

This case involves personnel administration. The principal, Dr. David Thompson, has been administering schools for 12 years, just completing his second year in the current position. The school enrolls 410 students. The problematic situation began in the spring, when one of the fourth-grade teachers announced that she would be retiring in the coming June. The standard way of filling a position in the district was to list the position as a transfer for other teachers in the district. However, two sixth-grade teachers at this school were interested in the position. The district's personnel director asked that the principal notify him about all vacancies by mid-May. The principal could not comply for two reasons. The first reason had to do with delays associated with figuring out the retiring teacher's retirement benefits, only after which the retirement would become official. The second reason related to the lack of closure on the issue of which of the two sixth-grade teachers, if any, to choose for the vacating fourth grade. If neither were chosen, then a new fourth-grade teacher would have to transfer from another school. If one of them were chosen, then a transfer to a sixth-grade class would be needed.

The principal decided to observe and participate in the problematic situation. He examined several dimensions of the situation and deliberated primarily on his own. The only input he received from others at this stage was from a female sixth grade teacher who informed him in March that she was interested in the position, and from a male sixth-grade teacher who, a few weeks later, stated that he was interested, too. The only demand on the principal was from the district's personnel director. The specific problematic issues the principal contemplated focused on his predisposition to appoint the female teacher to the fourth-grade position and to leave the male teacher in the sixth grade because he was more needed there as a mentor teacher. The principal wanted to separate the two teachers anyway because they did not work well as a team.

Dr. Thompson identified the two teachers and himself as the participants in the issues and also as those who were responsible for the issues. One very specific problem he would have would be the ill feelings he would create in the male teacher should he not be chosen for the fourth-grade position. The principal also thought of the possibility that the male teacher might leave, which would be unfortunate because he considered him to be an effective teacher. In the principal's mind, the two teachers and himself constituted the owners of the problem. This problem was the highest on the principal's priority list at that time of the year. He thought that the problem was also high on the priority list of both teachers. The female teacher wanted to teach in the fourth grade in order to be able to plan for classes along with her husband, who was also a fourth-grade teacher in another school. The male teacher wanted fourth-grade experience because he aspired to become an administrator. The principal viewed the effects of the problems, if they continued, as not terribly damaging as long as a choice between those two teachers was not made. He also saw no difficulties in managing the problems.

The problem he chose to work on was: Which of the two sixth-grade teachers should move to the vacant fourth-grade

position? There were two alternative solutions and three owners of the potential solutions. At this point the principal asked
for input. He wanted to know how truly important the move
was for both teachers. He detected emotional elements in the
male teacher's response, along with an extremely strong desire
to move. He had known that the female teacher also strongly
wanted to make the move. Dr. Thompson knew that the person
who was not selected would be extremely disappointed. He
viewed these possible negative effects as constituting a high
cost. He thought he could manage it either way, nonetheless.

The principal chose to transfer the female teacher to the
fourth grade. He informed her in a leisurely manner and she
reacted with joy. He informed the male teacher of the decision
in a hurried way and he was visibly upset. The principal felt
that these two interactions did not proceed effectively and that
he could have used better interpersonal skills. The cost was not
high, though. The principal felt that he alone owned this part
of the process. Following this, he did not find it necessary to
develop or implement a design for monitoring the implementation of the solution he chose.

CASE #3

When a Tenured Teacher Needs
to Improve Performance

This principal, Dr. Nancy Bergsahl, has been a principal for
7 years. She is now in her third year in the current school, where
enrollment is 460 students. Dr. Bergsahl faced a personnel case.
After 2 years of working with a weak third-grade teacher and
giving her poor evaluations, the principal has detected no significant improvement in her teaching. She feels that the teacher
should not have been hired in the first place. The teacher's
inadequacy has required frequent monitoring of her classroom
behavior, particularly because she disliked little boys. She appeared to discipline them for no justifiable reason. This teacher
had five students less in her classroom than the average class

enrollment in the school. The problematic situation became more complex early in the school year when the mother of one of the boys complained about the teacher. The principal thought that the mother was right, but at the same time she did not think that the teacher was poor enough to terminate. Dr. Bergsahl did not feel that she could be completely honest with the parent, however, and tell her about the problems with the other boys.

The principal decided to observe and participate in the problematic situation. She gave it quite a bit of thought. The major issue for her was to take care of the student who had emotional problems. Another issue was to deal with the teacher. The principal contemplated the origin of the issues. The teacher did not like teaching. The student came from a dysfunctional home. Although the principal believed that she, the teacher, the parent, and the child were participants in the issue, she considered only herself as responsible. The specific problem that the principal thought she should work on was the teacher's inability to teach. This was both the teacher's and her problem. For the teacher, to improve was not a high priority. For the principal, it was the highest priority. Other parents complained about the teacher, too. Dr. Bergsahl did not think that she could deal with these problems without the help of other teachers, some of whom had discussed the problem with her.

Dr. Bergsahl decided to work on the problem of changing the teacher's behavior from hostility to accepting boys as learners in her classroom. The principal met with several teachers a number of times. Three teachers offered to help. Two fifth/sixth-grade teachers met with the principal to brainstorm how to help, and one third-grade teacher met with her about how to deal with the teacher regarding specific items. The teacher rejected the help, whereupon the principal insisted on it. The third-grade teacher was to help with the curriculum. One fifth/sixth-grade teacher was going to become a mentor.

The principal viewed these possible solutions as her solutions. She considered them to be of the highest priority. She did not know what the effects of the solutions might be. She hoped for the best. The cost was going to involve released time and substitutes for the teacher, the mentor, and the other third-grade teacher. The principal consulted the district's director of personnel, the assistant superintendent, and the superintendent, too. She knew that if there were no improvement, the teacher would have to be terminated.

Dr. Bergsahl decided on the solution involving the two teachers. The teachers and she were in close communication. The teachers found the process a bit difficult because they were colleagues of the teacher but were now placed in the position of her evaluators. They liked supporting the principal, however. No one knew whether or not pressure would change the teacher. Beginning in January, the principal met with the teacher once a week, observing her attitudes and classroom behavior. The principal met with parents, too. The effects were noticeable. There were overt changes in the teacher's behavior. The teacher now seemed to be motivated because she wanted all of these people to leave her alone. The principal's evaluation at the time was that the change was moderately successful. This solution kept the principal quite busy, meeting frequently with the teacher, the two supporting teachers, the mother of the student, and the student, as well as with other students and their parents in this teacher's class. Dr. Bergsahl received support from the personnel director and the superintendent. The dollar cost of the solution implementation amounted to seven substitute days (three for the teacher and two each for the supporting teachers). The owners of the solution implementation process were the principal and the two supporting teachers.

The principal decided on a monitoring solution implementation design. It involved one hour per week of observing the teacher, including a follow-up meeting from time to time with the supporting teachers, discussions with the mother, and discussion with the student. The cost of implementing this design was time but also some frustration and anger. The principal felt that the improvement proceeded too slowly. The effectiveness of the monitoring involved stress for the teacher. It also took the principal away from other things that needed her attention. On the other hand, the two supporting teachers experienced satisfaction and so did the student's mother.

CASE #4

When Transfer Students Cause Staffing Problems

In this case, the principal, Mrs. Connie Zwortlie, had been administering schools for 11 years. She came to the current school 2 years ago, a school that enrolls 410 students. A substantial number of pupils were high-quality transfer students. The school itself had experienced declining enrollment for several years, primarily because of the small number of families with school-age children residing in this upper-middle-class section of town. The principal approached the school site council and her teachers in group meetings and concluded that the problematic issue was made up of three interrelated parts. The first was how to continue to support transfer students. The second was how to maintain an adequate student-teacher ratio without losing a teacher. The third was how to avoid grade-combination classes. If fewer students were allowed to transfer into the school, a combination class could be avoided, but the school would lose a teacher. If more students were accepted as transfers, the school would avoid losing a teacher but there would have to be a combination class. This case involved issues of personnel, student personnel, and budget.

The principal decided to observe and participate in the problematic situation. She studied the origin of the issues in depth. She talked to the superintendent and the assistant superintendent, as well as to her teaching staff. Mrs. Zwortlie found out that the school's last two principals had not lost any teachers while also controlling the admission of high-quality transfer students. She also found out that both principals had exercised strong, aggressive leadership with not much shared decision making. This principal felt strongly that in a district in which power was significantly decentralized and schools were empowered to make many decisions, her style of leadership was suitable. She was used to sharing most of the decision-making process with the teaching staff and the school site council. Her problem was that in such situations, empowerment must be greater than it was. Budgets would also have to decentralized.

She felt that principals should be able to decide on the number of teachers they must have.

Mrs. Zwortlie considered on her own several items. She felt that herself, her full staff, and the site council were participants in the issues and that she alone was responsible for them. She realized that the three-part issue mentioned previously as the possible specific problem was the one she should work on. She met with her staff and site council several times about it, feeling that all three parties should own this problem and that the problem should be at the top of the priority list of all three of them. After again meeting with these two groups, Mrs. Zwortlie identified the possible lingering effects of the problem. A wedge was being driven between transfer and nontransfer students. The manageability problem that she saw centered around the school's unreliable enrollment figures. As it turned out, the district did not have such information either. Knowing that the district and not the school controlled the purse further increased pressure on her.

In midyear the principal decided to gamble on high enrollment figures and to work on the resulting problems. She talked to the assistant superintendent and to the superintendent about the need to retain a teacher at all costs and to avoid combination classes. She informed parents about the possibility of not continuing their children's transfer status. This alternative solution brought quite a bit of pressure on her. At this point she saw the district office personnel and herself as potential owners of the solutions. The problem was at the top of their priority list. The possible effects of the March mailing that she sent to parents of transfer students intensified the pressure. The cost was also high with the teaching staff, who in April still did not know about their assignment for the following year.

Mrs. Zwortlie decided on a solution and she implemented it. The solution depended on both the final enrollment figures and the superintendent's decision. The enrollment figures were seven students short of the target, but the superintendent approved one smaller class, removing the need for a combination class. Thus, there was no need to lose a teacher. The solution implementation process proceeded well. The principal felt that the effectiveness of the process was high, its manageability difficult, due to lack of control over money at the school level, and its cost was high in terms of time and pressure. Throughout the solution implementation process she felt that herself, the district office leadership, her teaching staff, and her school site council were the owners of the solution process.

She now monitored the solution implementation. Mrs. Zwortlie had already thought about the deficiencies of the present empowerment situation. She also observed that the teaching staff was beginning to look at the school as a whole collective. She felt that the process was worthwhile despite the deficiencies. The cost of teachers now monitoring more things was not high; it was in accord with the principal's leadership style. It was still too early to determine the effectiveness of the monitoring.

The Conducting of Administrative
Evaluations by Middle School Principals

CASE #5

When Too Many Bright and Ethnically Diverse
Students Desire Placement in Class for the Gifted

This middle school is composed of grades seven and eight and has 620 students. The principal, Mr. Frank Trujillo, has been an administrator for 28 years, 17 of them in the current school. There is also another administrator at the school, an assistant principal. Prior to the beginning of each school year, the principal experienced pressure from parents to enroll their children in the school's gifted and talented (GATE) program. The problematic situation was two-fold. First, the number of requests on behalf of qualified youngsters was twice as large as the number of GATE spots available. Requests on behalf of 120 seventh graders and 180 eighth graders had to be turned down. Also, two conflicting philosophies had emerged among people involved with GATE and GATE-related issues at the school. Those parents whose children were accepted to GATE, as well as teachers and others who worked with GATE students, believed in homogeneous grouping of talented students. Parents and teachers who lobbied to improve the quality of the *entire* school believed in heterogeneous groups. Issues were interwoven with each other here. There were issues of governance, instruction, curriculum, personnel, student personnel, budget, and school-community relations.

The principal decided to observe and participate in the problematic situation. After consulting with teachers, counselors, and district office personnel, he sorted out the problematic issues as follows: First, there were twice as many students in the school who qualified for the GATE English and social studies classes as there were available spots (60 spots in each grade level). There were also twice as many students in the school who qualified for the GATE mathematics classes as there were available spots (60 spots in each grade level). In addition, there were twice as many eligible students as available spots (60 spots) for eighth-grade GATE science. The competition for GATE programs was strong. The effect on rejected students was unfortunate. The principal detected one central origin of these issues. It was the desire of parents to materialize aspirations that they and their children had. Participants in these issues were the principal, a counselor whose role was to make recommendations about placement of students who were new to the school, and a few teachers whose role was to make placement recommendations about continuing students. The principal and the counselor were responsible for the issues; the principal established GATE admission policy guidelines and the counselor implemented those guidelines.

Mr. Trujillo believed that it would be beneficial to work on two specific strategic problems. One was the reexamination of criteria used to admit students to GATE programs, particularly the lowest 20% of the applicants. Typically, the principal and the counselor together made the decisions to admit them. (The other 80% were admitted by the counselor alone, according to the principal's guidelines.) The other possible problem was to examine what alternative could be offered to those students whose applications to GATE classes were denied. These problems were top priority for the principal and for the counselor.

Possible effects of not solving the problems were going to be significant—pedagogic and political effects, especially. The principal saw no problems in the manageability of these two problems.

The principal decided to work on these two problems. His goal for the first problem was to increase diversity among GATE students. His goal for the second problem was to improve the quality of education for those who were qualified but not accepted into the GATE classes.

After consulting extensively with several groups, the principal thought of two respective possible solutions. First, he thought that the diversity criterion should be included among those used for considering students for GATE. Second, he thought of creating honor classes that would enroll GATE-qualified-but-denied-students and that would offer enrichment and opportunity for accelerated learning. He believed that the counselor and himself (on appeal cases only) were the owners of these possible solutions and that both of them would also view the possible solutions as top priority. Mr. Trujillo also thought that these possible solutions would increase satisfaction for parents and challenges for students, enhance a favorable racial balance in the school, and renew motivation for some of the teachers. The cost of these possible solutions ($50 per GATE student) would have to be allocated from the district office. There would be political costs, too, of changing the criteria for admission. On the basis of discussions about these proposed solutions with parents, the school site GATE committee, and other groups, the principal had come to believe that the manageability of the proposed solutions would be feasible.

He decided on these two solutions. He evaluated their implementation process and found that the process began satisfactorily. The potential effectiveness of the process was high due to the proportional racial representation in GATE and to the wide initial participation in the honor classes, too. In the latter, enrichment was offered to the students, particularly in mathematics in the seventh grade. The political loss, according to the principal, was not low. Some mathematics teachers who taught the honor classes were interested in acceleration (like GATE) rather than enrichment. All of this was done without extra monetary cost. The principal and the counselor remained owners of the solution implementation process.

The principal chose a solution implementation monitoring design and implemented it. He selected the student achievement scores as his key indicator for the program's success but incurred the cost of time, though, because it involved spending quite a bit of time with these scores. Scores derived from both GATE classes and the honor classes were analyzed. Teachers in the school who were considered effective and dedicated informed the principal on a regular basis about their perceptions of the meaning of the scores. The principal considered his monitoring activities to be effective.

CASE #6

When the Afternoon Detention Hall
Is Overcrowded

The principal, Mr. Victor Dubinsky, has administered this current school for 9 years. The school enrolls 610 students and also has an assistant principal. The problematic situation involved mounting numbers of students (overload) in the afternoon detention hall, the inability to explain why, and the inability to tell whether anything was wrong with the discipline system. The case involved student personnel and budgeting issues. The principal decided to observe and participate in this problematic situation.

The principal asked for data from the detention supervisor. He also asked the secretary to classify the cases by causes. He found that there were too many students in detention (usually 20, but up to 52; usually 400 per semester, but up to 300 cases in only 6 weeks). He also found out that one half of them were there for disciplinary behavior and the rest for tardiness, lack of preparation for class, uncovered books, and failure to attend lunch or classroom detention. The principal conjectured that the origin of these problematic issues could be a decrease in teacher control of students. He considered the detention supervisor and the Saturday work supervisor as participating in these issues, along with the students, the teachers, the parents, and himself. Those responsible for the issues were himself, the students, and the teachers.

Mr. Dubinsky approached individual teachers and the faculty advisory committee (FAC) to discuss possible specific problems to work on. They looked at student behavior, criteria for detention, and teacher attitude and style. Owners of these problems were those who participated in the problematic issues. As top priority the principal wanted a better school climate. The teachers' top priorities were clear consequences for students and improvement in student behavior. The students wanted time for socializing and citizenship points. If the problems lingered, teacher morale would suffer and there would be additional problems with students. The manageability of the problems was considered satisfactory if a shared decision-making arrangement could be maintained.

The principal decided to work on the problems of criteria for detention, student behavior, and teacher authorities with regard to choices of punishment. Working with FAC and considering many dimensions on his own, the principal thought of the following possible solutions: Restructure criteria for detention to include only disruptive behavior; use alternative discipline methods for tardiness; and encourage teachers in the process. He considered all of the earlier participants in the problematic issues, as well as those involved in the problems chosen to be worked on, as additional owners of the possible solutions. The owners' top priorities included time to socialize for the students, improved student conduct for the teachers, and improved teacher morale for the principal. All felt that the effects of these solutions would be positive. The cost would include money for supervisors, time for in-service for teachers and staff, and mail communication to students and parents. The principal believed that the solutions could be manageable.

Subsequently, Mr. Dubinsky decided on implementing revised criteria for detention, communicating them to all concerned, and also implementing some other disciplinary actions for tardiness and nondisruptive offenses. He consulted with FAC and its subcommittee, communicated to them the decisions, and initiated a staff and teacher in-service workshop on the new criteria. He expected the effectiveness to be high. He was not sure about most aspects of manageability.

The principal considered on his own a monitoring solution implementation design. He chose quarterly reports on incidents of detention and the reasons for them. He also requested a breakdown of these data by each teacher. The cost was only that of time. The monitoring effectiveness was high.

The Conducting of Administrative Evaluations by Assistant High School Principals

CASE #7

When Interracial Physical Violence Erupts

The assistant principal, Mr. Jeffrey Takai, has been in high school administration for the past 18 years, all at the current school, with 12 of those years in the current position. The school includes grades 9 through 12. It enrolls 1,240 students, 39% of whom are minorities, with two thirds of those being of Hispanic origin.

In the past few years Mr. Takai had observed some results of the significant rise in the Hispanic student population. Most teachers were unable to adopt to the new situation. Interracial physical conflicts among the students had intensified. Gangs were forming and fighting each other. The principal asked Mr. Takai to handle this situation. Both of them saw here curricular issues, personnel and student personnel issues, and school-community relations issues. The assistant principal first decided to observe and participate in the situation in order to understand it better.

The school district officials discussed this situation, which had also appeared in the other high schools in the district. The assistant principal did not feel that these discussions were helpful to him in solving the problems on his campus. He began a round of discussions with several individuals in the school and in the community. Then he explored the issues with the school's administrative and counseling teams. He was concerned with the issues of who should be approaching the gang members and with what messages. He believed that the origins of the issues were the racial differences among the students and the lack of familiarity between racial groups.

At the beginning, the assistant principal had no help in facing these issues. Most teachers in this school did not want to be involved. He became the sole person responsible for the situation.

After talking to numerous students, the assistant principal began thinking about organizing a group of students who would serve as a link between himself and the gangs. Specific problems in this connection would include the questions of who should participate in the group, how participants were to be elected, how they were to be trained, what they would be asked to do, how their safety would be ensured, and how they would be viewed by others in the school.

The assistant principal discussed these possible problems with eight individuals. They included the principal, the English-as-a-second-language teacher, four regular classroom teachers, a counselor who was on the permanent staff, and a temporary counselor whose position was funded by a grant. These eight individuals, together with the assistant principal, became owners of these possible problems. They viewed the containment of gang fighting as their top priority. None of these nine individuals were able to predict at the time what effects the choice of these possible problems would have or how manageable the problems might be.

Mr. Takai decided to work on forming a class he called the leadership class. He recruited students from the 10th, 11th, and 12th grades, but most (70%) were 12th graders. He handpicked a total of 45 students. To him, they represented the school as a whole and he told them so. He also informed them that he wanted them to be of service to the school—specifically to be the direct link between himself and the gang members. At the beginning, most students in the leadership class were confused about their roles. Some were afraid. Others were eager to help but did not know how. Many were passive and silent.

At that point he consulted heavily with his secretary, the head of the social studies department, and the potential guest lecturers for the leadership class. He chose assimilation as the theme for the class. Guest lecturers supplemented his own presentations. There were also many extracurricular activities. The assistant principal ended up being the sole owner of this possible set of solutions. He considered them to be his highest priorities. He believed that the effects would be positive: The students' roles as leaders would be accepted, and physical fights might diminish. The cost of these solutions would include a portion of the personnel involved plus $5,000 per year raised from private sources. The assistant principal felt that this set of possible solutions would be manageable.

His chosen solution was the establishment of the leadership class, an elective that met during fourth period. The assistant principal continuously consulted with the head of the social studies department and with his secretary. He selected the guest lecturers, who explained to the leadership class different dimensions of assimilation and also showed ways of approaching gang members. Mr. Takai predicted that the success of the class would be high, with the exception of the complaints of the Caucasian student class members who still had a hard time understanding their role. The manageability of the solution implementation process was satisfactory. The costs were as projected. The assistant principal felt that the owners of the solution implementation process included himself, his two close advisers, and the guest lecturers.

Mr. Takai decided to monitor the solution implementation process. After consulting with his immediate advisers and with the guest lecturers, he designed and implemented monitoring procedures that included the following: Every Monday he and his close advisers evaluated information the students reported about their contacts with the gang members. The assistant principal personally would also solicit reactions and responses from the student body as a whole, the gang members, and teachers. Results indicated that over a 3-year duration the offerings in the leadership class had improved, the percentage of leadership class students sensing ownership of the project had increased (80% in 1991-1992), the number of teachers approving of the class and the results had also increased (75% in 1991-1992), and most important, the number of incidents of racial physical violence had decreased (by 50% in 3 years).

CASE #8

When a Grant Is Needed to Restructure a School

The assistant principal, Mrs. Diane Hollingsworth, has administered this school for 6 years. The school enrolls 2,300 students and there are three other assistant principals as well. The problematic situation included several problems with student behavior and student achievement and the need for massive financial aid to restructure the curriculum, instruction, and governance of the school. Altogether, there were issues of governance, instruction, curriculum, personnel, budget, student personnel, and school-community relations. The assistant principal decided to observe and participate in the problematic situation.

First she discussed the issues with the school's program coordinators (PCs), the school-based management team (SBMT), teachers, and parents. She determined that student achievement scores were low, college enrollment rates of graduates were low, absenteeism rates were high, and transiency rates were high. Mrs. Hollingsworth consulted the school site program evaluators (SSPE) and teachers and learned that the origin of the issues was apparent in the data that the school had collected in the past (CTBS scores, local colleges surveys, school attendance reports, and registrar's accumulated data). She saw the PCs as participants in these issues and considered the district and school curriculum planners, as well as the school administrators and teachers, responsible for these issues. The possible problems she chose to work on included raising student achievement scores and college enrollment and decreasing absenteeism and transiency rates. Teachers and parents told her that district and school administrators were the owners of these problems. She agreed. Their priority was to write a grant in order to obtain funding to work on these problems. She perceived dangerous effects if the problems lingered. Mrs. Hollingsworth considered the manageability of these problems without extramural funding as almost impossible.

The assistant principal decided to work on the problems of student achievement, college attendance, absenteeism, and transiency. She met with the SBMT to formulate a plan and discuss it with teachers and parents. The possible solution of the chosen problems was to write a grant proposal to fund major school restructuring that would then facilitate achievement and decrease absenteeism. After meeting with the SBMT, parents, and teachers, Mrs. Hollingsworth determined that the owners of this possible solution would be herself, the faculty, the chair of the union's association in the school, a parent/community representative, and the community. She also realized that the priority of all of the solution owners would be to obtain funds for a major restructuring through the writing of a grant proposal. What would be needed was to write the proposal, hope for the funds, and then implement the plan, if funded.

The assistant principal then met with the administrators to find out what they believed would happen. They thought that the solution would have an impact on student achievement, future college enrollment, and absenteeism. The administration also felt that the cost of the solution would be in the following areas: staff development/evaluation, community outreach, and equipment/technology/services. After discussions with the personnel director and others in the school the assistant principal perceived that moving authority to the school site, including authority of purchasing and expenditures, would simplify the manageability of the solution. The district office was to continue to audit the accounts.

Mrs. Hollingsworth decided on a major restructuring of curriculum content and instructional format. She also decided on restructuring the governance of the school. She met with prospective owners of the solution to write the grant proposal. Evaluators told her that the impact would be very positive. She established a central management council (CMC) to manage the solution, including the budget, the curriculum, discipline, and staffing. Costs would be as planned. The revised ownership list of the solution included the principal, the SBMT, the CMC, teachers, and parents.

The assistant principal decided on a solution monitoring design. The SBMT would be in charge of the monitoring process. Six instruments were to be developed and/or used: test scores, student opinion surveys, staff opinion polls, parent opinion surveys, instruments developed by the CMC, and independent outside evaluations. Mrs. Hollingsworth met with the solution owners and assigned monitoring responsibilities. The main costs were going to be for the independent outside evaluators. The assistant principal thought that periodic assessments would make the monitoring process highly effective.

The Conducting of Administrative Evaluations by High School Principals

CASE #9

When the Father of a Suspended Student Charges Racial Discrimination

In this case the principal, Dr. Darren Von Shpies, had been in his present job for 8 years. The school enrolls 1,675 students, includes grades 9 through 12, and has three assistant principals. The principal's problematic situation involved two students on the football team who were caught fighting. One student hit the other, who did not hit back. The one who did the hitting was suspended; the other one was not. The parent of the student who was suspended accused the principal of racial discrimination. This case involved student personnel issues and school issues associated with the school-community relations. He decided to observe and participate in the problematic situation.

Dr. Von Shpies followed up after a phone call from the assistant principal. He talked to the students, the parents, and to witnesses. The problematic issues he discovered were focused on the fairness of this treatment, the possible racial issues, the consistency in imposing school rules, and parent involvement. He reviewed disciplinary records and checked with the assistant principal on the origin of the issues. Everything seemed to point to the poor impulse control of the student who did the hitting. The principal believed that the participants in the issues and those responsible included himself, the assistant principal, the coach, the players, the students involved, the witnesses, and the parents. Based on additional discussions, he saw four possible specific problems he could work on: student aggression, fairness in treating students, satisfying the parent, and racial discrimination. The owners of these problems were to include himself, the student who hit, the coach, and the parent. For the student, the top priority would be to reduce aggression. The priority for the principal would be to demonstrate fairness. For the coach, the top priority would be to help in aggression reduction. For the father, the priority would be ensuring fair treatment. Dr. Von Shpies checked with the written school policy and saw that continued aggression would lead to more severe punishment. Also, if there were no demonstration of fair treatment, the issue would go to the school board, resulting in negative consequences. He also predicted that problem management might have an impact on not only the student but also the football team and the school.

The principal decided to work on two problems. One was the student's aggression. The other was the claims of unfairness from the parent and the student. He chose the following possible solutions to the first problem: Enforce the suspension, counsel the coach and the special education teacher about teaching alternative strategies, and reduce suspension as had been requested by the parent. He chose these three possibilities as a result of consulting the written school rules and talking with the coach and the special education teacher. The possible solutions he chose for the second problem were: gathering written evidence, maintaining consistency according to school rules, and meeting with the parent. He chose these possibilities as a result of discussions with all participants. The principal saw himself, the student, the coach, the special education teacher, the parent, and witnesses as owners of these two possible solutions. The priorities varied. His was consistency in applying the rules. The student's and parent's priorities were fair treatment and suggested alternatives. For the coach and the teacher the priority was the teaching of alternative solutions. The effects of the possible solutions included getting the student's attention, improving his impulse control, satisfying the parent, and communicating consistency to the rest of the team. The principal saw everyone's time as a cost. He also considered the cost of losing a key player. The principal saw no problems with manageability of the possible solutions.

Dr. Von Shpies's chosen solutions were to suspend the student for the appropriate length of time, to prove that this was fair treatment to the parent, and to consult with the coach and special education teacher on proactive strategies. He discussed the implementation process with the assistant principal and the coach. The suspension forms were completed and processed, and meetings took place with the coach and teacher on one hand and the parent on the other. In the principal's judgment, the suspension process was effective, the discussions with the coach and teacher were on their way, and the meeting with the parent involved effective sharing of the pertinent documentation. Dr. Von Shpies thought that the solution implementation process was manageable but costly in terms of people's time. He also thought that the owners of the solutions included himself, the coach, the teacher, the parent, and the student.

The principal decided to design and implement a monitoring solution implementation system. He included in it the examination of time spent by the coach and the special education teacher. It also included the constant watching of the student. Effectiveness, he thought, was high. The monitoring system showed increased effectiveness of the efforts of the coach and the teacher and increased impulse control on the part of the student.

CASE #10

When a Teacher Is Beaten by a Student

This was the first year on the job for this principal, Mr. Herbert Shezeik. His school includes grades 9 through 12. It enrolls 650 students and has two assistant principals. The problematic situation involved a fight during lunchtime in which two seniors participated. A teacher who attempted to stop the fight was beaten by one of the students. The issue was primarily a student personnel issue. The principal decided to observe and participate in the problematic situation. Checking with various witnesses, he verified that both students were involved in the fight, but only one hit the teacher. Checking further with the students and parents, he found that the origin of the incident stemmed from a summer altercation. Clearly there were three participants in the issues. The principal held the students and their parents responsible for what happened. The possible problems the principal considered to work on were to determine whether to expel the student who struck the teacher and also to determine the consequences for the other student.

Mr. Shezeik determined quickly that he was the owner of these possible problems. His priorities were to act quickly, to send a message to the student body, and to restore any authority that had been challenged. He thought that the effects would be good if he acted quickly. He knew that he had the support of the superintendent in his management of the problem. As it turned out, the principal ultimately decided to determine whether to expel the student who struck the teacher and to suspend the other student.

The principal and his aides felt that the possible solution needed to be implemented quickly. He saw himself as the owner of the possible solution. His priority to do it was high. Mr. Shezeik cared about the effects of the possible solution, especially on future violence and order in the school. He and his aides saw no monetary cost to this possible solution except in terms of staff time. The principal considered the possible solution to be quite manageable if implemented, because the procedural guidelines were clear.

Mr. Shezeik then decided to expel the student who hit the teacher and to suspend the other one. Once the decision was made, the implementation process proceeded fairly easily. It was highly effective, due to the cooperation of the administrators, teachers, and the superintendent. It was manageable, involving only time as a cost, and the owners included the principal and his aides. The principal did not see any need to monitor the solution implementation.

4

IMPROVING PRACTICE:
SYNTHESIZING THE CASES

The intent of this chapter is to help school administrators improve their involvement with administrative evaluation. The tools selected here are syntheses of data derived from the 30 interviews. Patterns and examples of these data are used in connection with specifying problematic situations, highlighting consistency among key decisions made in these situations, and helping readers become acquainted with dominant methodologies used in evaluation as an administrative function. First the chapter presents syntheses of data about the problematic situations and the role of administrative evaluation in these situations. These syntheses are followed by other syntheses related to the four key decisions in each problematic situation and, again, the role of evaluation in these decisions. Last, the chapter discusses syntheses of the 22 sets of administrative evaluations themselves, particularly those focused on the evaluation methodologies.

Problematic Situations
and the Use of Administrative Evaluation

All of the 30 administrators who were interviewed identified a problematic situation that they had experienced. Their choices mirrored their major concerns. Collectively, their choices represent situations that typically occur in elementary and secondary schools in California and in the nation. Together, these choices deal with most of the administrative domains known in the literature (e.g., Kimbrough & Nunnery, 1988). The domains included in the cases are governance, curriculum, instruction, personnel, student personnel, budget, and school-community relations. Table 4.1 summarizes the 30 cases; Chapter 3 discusses cases 1 through 10; cases 11 through 30 are in Resource A.

Table 4.1 shows that not all cases involve the same administrative domains. For example, 5 cases involved governance issues and 9 cases involved the curriculum. The budget and instruction were associated with 11 cases each. Issues of school-community relations involved 14 cases. Personnel issues and student personnel issues were associated with 22 cases. Personnel cases were frequently associated with cases mentioned by the six assistant high school principals. Student personnel cases were often associated with cases mentioned by high school principals.

From another perspective, Table 4.1 shows that most of the 30 administrative cases simultaneously involved three to five administrative domains. Five cases involved all seven domains. Those cases included image building (elementary principal), accelerated learning (middle school principal), noncompliance with a bilingual plan (middle school principal), a disabled student (assistant high school principal), and a grant for restructuring (assistant high school principal). None of the cases mentioned by any high school principal involved all seven domains. To be associated with issues in more than one or two administrative domains is to deal with complexity. Issues of different natures are interwoven with each other, making solutions difficult to accept. Table 4.1 does not include maintenance and support service domains. None of the 30 cases chosen were associated with these issues.

All 30 school administrators perceived the problematic situations that they chose for the interview as at least somewhat serious.

(*text continues on page 70*)

TABLE 4.1 The 30 Cases by Administrative Domain

#	Case	Governance	Curriculum	Instruction	Personnel	Student personnel	Budget	School community relations
1	Parents & the bilingual class			X				X
2	Teaching vacancy				X			
3	Teacher improvement				X			
4	Empowerment				X	X	X	
5	Accelerated learning	X	X	X	X	X	X	X
6	Overloaded detention hall					X	X	
7	Interracial physical violence		X		X	X		X

8	Needed grant	X	X	X	X	X	X	X
9	A suspension and racial discrimination charges					X		X
10	Teacher is beaten in a student fight					X		
11	Combination classes			X	X	X	X	
12	Uncertain student numbers				X	X	X	
13	Split staff		X		X			
14	Blame the home			X		X		X
15	Image changing	X	X	X	X	X	X	X
16	Parents and reputedly weak teachers				X	X		X
17	Ineffective assistant				X			

(continued)

TABLE 4.1 Continued

#	Case	Governance	Curriculum	Instruction	Personnel	Student personnel	Budget	School community relations
18	Disabled teacher			X	X		X	
19	Students march		X			X		X
20	Excessive student misbehavior				X	X		
21	A student's unacceptable behavior					X		
22	Noncompliance with a bilingual plan	X	X	X	X	X	X	X
23	Needed cuts			X	X		X	

#								
24	Attendance policy is resisted					X	X	
25	A disabled student	X		X	X	X	X	X
26	Class overload		X	X	X	X		
27	Facing negative publicity			X	X	X		X
28	Absence of leadership			X	X			X
29	A suspension and a complaint			X	X			X
30	Interference with staff involvement		X					

As the interview unfolded, their perceptions of how central their role was in the situation reflected just how seriously they really did perceive the situation to be. Heavy involvement was associated with a perception that the situation was quite serious. Their increased clarity of perception about the seriousness of the problematic situation involved progressive specificity of the situation itself. The specificity was greatly enhanced by heavy engagement in evaluation. Following are some relevant items in the interview protocol.

The interview protocol included four items that described the problematic situation as follows:

1. the original statement of the problematic situation;
2. (following decision A to face and observe the problematic situation) administrative evaluation item #1: problematic issues;
3. administrative evaluation item #5: possible specific problems to work on; and
4. decision B: problem to work on.

The original intent of items 2, 3, and 4 afforded the interviewees the opportunity to add to the original description. Tables 4.2, 4.3, 4.4, and 4.5 contain five examples of these complete descriptions of each problematic situation.

In all five cases depicted in Tables 4.2, 4.3, 4.4, and 4.5:

1. The original statement of the problematic situation is broad (e.g., resistance to combination classes, changing the school image, overloaded detention hall, cuts, racial discrimination); and
2. The decision statement B regarding the problem to work on is more specific (e.g., imposing a curriculum, helping weak teachers to improve, specific criteria for detention, correcting student-teacher ratios, reducing student aggression).

It is highly likely that this progressive move toward specificity is facilitated by the two intervening evaluations (#A.1 and #A.5) in which the following was identified:

1. the object to be evaluated;
2. the methodology of evaluation; and

3. the evaluation findings.

Another useful benefit of these two evaluations is that they help identify indicators for detecting additional issues and problems, as well as solutions. Examples of indicators include, respectively, unhealthy parental competition for teachers, unenthusiastic teachers, 50% of students in detention are there for disruptive behavior, too many students in social studies classes, and parental involvement. Such evaluations involve informational as well as judgmental dimensions.

Most of the 30 administrators made use of the complete description (four items) of the problematic situation primarily because the interviewer asked them to do so. It is difficult to tell how many principals would do so in their actual work. One may surmise that the more school administrators made use of these four items (and especially the two that represent evaluation), the easier it might be for them to proceed with subsequent decisions and additional evaluations.

Key Decisions and Administrative
Use of Evaluation

It is, perhaps, customary to think of decisions in school administration as specific actions taken by administrators for the purpose of correcting or rectifying problems. This book certainly adopts this posture as well. The book also assumes, however, that decisions in school administration relate to finding solutions. Thus the interview protocol includes four such decisions: to face and observe the problematic situation, to choose a problem to work on, to choose a solution and implement it, and to choose a system of solution implementation monitoring and implement it. The first two and a half decisions relate to change only; the last one and a half to solutions. Tables 4.6, 4.7, 4.8, and 4.9 summarize the second, third, and fourth decisions in each of the 30 cases described in this book. Collectively, the decisions and the 22 evaluations scattered among them captured the entire problem-solving process in each case.

Tables 4.6, 4.7, 4.8, and 4.9 show that 23 of the 30 school administrators reported having made all the decisions. Seven administrators

(text continues on page 77)

TABLE 4.2 Issues or Problems in the Case of Elementary School Principals

Selected items appearing in the instrument	Issues or problems	
	"When teachers do not want combination classes" (Case #11)	"When the principal believes that the school's image requires change" (Case #15)
The problematic situation	1. The teaching staff is not the principal's. 2. Competition among the staff. 3. The staff refuses to take on combination classes. 4. Two combination classes are formed when only one is needed. 5. Parental complaints about #4 above. 6. A teacher refuses to use a handwriting program. 7. A teacher is not being a team player.	1. Low student achievement scores. 2. Poor teaching of 40% of the school's students attending bilingual classes.
Evaluative item #1 - The problematic issues	8. Unhealthy parental competition for teachers. 9. Lack of continuity in the curriculum. 10. Difficulties in building teachers' teams. 11. A teacher does not cooperate if the ideas are not hers.	3. Unenthusiastic teachers. 4. Racist attitude among teachers and community. 5. Community negative perception about teachers and school. 6. Lack of understanding of student achievement score. 7. White flight. 8. Lack of information about school.
Evaluative item #5 - Specific problems to work on	12. Lack of continuity in the curriculum. 13. Difficulties in promoting a special project involving 6th, 1st, and 2nd grades.	9. How teachers are seen. 10. How to increase the visibility of outstanding teachers. 11. How to help weak teachers improve. 12. How to inform the community about school.

		13. How to inform the real estate agents about the school.
Decision B - Choosing a problem to work on	14. How to impose a new spelling curriculum on an uncooperative combination class teacher.	14. Same as #10 above. 15. Same as #11 above. 16. Same as #12 above. 17. Same as #13 above.

TABLE 4.3 Issues or Problems in the Case of Middle School Principals

Selected items appearing in the instrument	Issues or problems *"When the afternoon detention hall is overloaded"* (Case #6)
The problematic situation	1. The afternoon detention hall is overloaded. 2. Unclear reasons as to why the overload. 3. Problems with the discipline system.
Evaluative item #1 - The problematic issues	4. Too many students in detention. 5. Fifty percent of the students in detention are there for disruptive behavior. 6. Fifty percent of the students in detention are there for tardiness, lack of preparation for class, uncovered books, or failure to attend lunch or classroom detention.
Evaluative item #5 - Possible specific problems to work on	7. Criteria for detention vs. other disciplinary problems are not clear. 8. Teacher attitudes toward detention are not clear.
Decision B - Choosing a problem to work on	9. Developing specific criteria for detention. 10. Developing specific criteria for student behavior. 11. Empowering teachers through alternatives.

TABLE 4.4 Issues or Problems in the Case of Assistant High School Principals

Selected items appearing in the instrument	*Issues or problems* *"When major cuts have to take place" (Case #23)*
The problematic situation	1. Nine classes and two substitute teachers had to be cut. 2. Too few classes in bilingual education. 3. Too many students in social studies classes.
Evaluative item #1 - The problematic issues	4. Student schedules disrupted. 5. Bilingual program disrupted. 6. Difficulty of getting the correct ratio of students to teachers in social studies classes. 7. Overstaffing.
Evaluative item #5 - Possible specific problems to work on	8. Which teachers and classes to cut. 9. Correct ratio in social studies class.
Decision B - Choosing a problem to work on	10. Correct ratio in social studies classes.

TABLE 4.5 Issues or Problems in the Case of High School Principals

Selected items appearing in the instrument	Issues or problems "When a father of a suspended student charges racial discrimination" (Case #9)
The problematic situation	1. Two football team players involved in a fight. 2. One student hit and was suspended. The other did not hit and was not suspended. 3. The parent of the student who hit accused the principal of racial discrimination.
Evaluative item #1 - The problematic issues	4. Was there fair treatment of the students? 5. Were these racial issues? 6. Are school rules imposed consistently? 7. Parent involvement.
Evaluative item #5 - Possible specific problems to work on	8. Aggression of student who hit. 9. Racial discrimination. 10. Fair treatment of all students. 11. Satisfying a parent.
Decision B - Choosing a problem to work on	12. Reducing student aggression. 13. Investigating claims of unfairness.

reported not having made the last decision (monitoring). These latter cases involved elementary school principals: #14 (blaming the home), #2 (a teaching vacancy), and #18 (disabled teacher); assistant high school principals: #26 (class overload); and high school principals: #27 (facing negative publicity), #29 (a suspension and a complaint), and #10 (teacher is beaten). In all seven cases the reported engagement in evaluation prior to decision D was heavy. Extensive engagement in evaluation during the problem-solving process may render the monitoring of the solution implementation unnecessary or, at most, low priority.

Another use of evaluation with regard to key decisions is associated with interdecisional relations. Two questions are of interest here:

1. How consistent are the decisions (B, C, D) with each other?
2. How clear is the relation between any two of them?

In several cases, evaluation produced pertinent information that enhanced the consistency between the decisions and also the clarity of their relationship. Case #1 in the elementary schools group (Table 4.6) is a good example of a clear, simple, and direct interdecisional relationship between decisions B, C, and D. The problematic case involved parents' attitudes toward bilingual classes. The decision (B) about what problem to work on was to create awareness in English-only parents of the value of bilingual classes for their children. The decision (C) about the solution was to convince these parents to enroll in a Spanish class themselves. The decision (D) about monitoring was to get feedback from parents and students about the students' progress. Another good example of clarity and consistency is case #25 in the assistant high school principals group (Table 4.8) in which the problematic situation was the enrollment of a disabled student without records. The decisions (B) about the problems to work on were to get the records, plan for the classes, and determine needed assistance. The decisions (C) about the solutions were to enroll in classes and assign an aide. The decision (D) about monitoring was to develop assessment responsibilities for appropriate staff.

In other cases the interdecisional relationship was found to be complex. In the main, the problem-solving process in such cases

(*text continues on page 84*)

TABLE 4.6 Decisions Made by Elementary School Principals

#	Case	Decision about problem	Decision about solution	Decision about monitoring
1	Parents and the bilingual class	To create awareness on the part of English-only parents about advantages for them if their children enrolled in a bilingual program.	To convince parents to enroll in a Spanish class.	To ask parents and teachers about student progress.
2	Teaching vacancy	Which 6th-grade teacher to appoint.	To appoint one of the 6th-grade teachers.	None.
3	Teacher improvement	To work on changing teacher behavior from hostility to acceptance.	To enlist the help of two of the school's teachers.	To observe the teacher.
4	Empowerment	To wait and see what the enrollment numbers will be.	To get teachers to agree unanimously that there should not be a combination class.	To ask teachers about their attitude toward shared decision making.
11	Combination classes	To introduce the new spelling program in the combination class.	To inform one teacher and work with her.	To ask other grade level teachers about the teacher's work.
12	Uncertain student numbers	To wait and see what enrollment numbers will be. To convince superintendent to give a teaching position (another teacher) in place of combination classes.	To create three combination classes.	To ask parents about their feelings. To have the school psychologist ask students about their feelings.

78

13	Split staff	To develop a program which enhances the integration of the two groups of students.	To initiate a school wide exchange program. To teach English to Spanish speakers and Spanish to English speakers.	To ask teachers to fill out an evaluation instrument.
14	Blame the home	To impress upon the teaching staff the learning needs of all children.	To create a staff development plan to address multicultural issues.	None.
15	Image changing	To work on the teachers' image. To improve the visibility of outstanding teachers. To improve weak teachers. To inform community and realtors about the school.	The same as decision about problem.	To ask two teachers to evaluate and inform the principal. To have the principal evaluate and inform the school site council.
16	Parents and reputedly weak teachers	To work on a student placement policies document.	To write a brochure that confirms student placement policies.	To ask teachers to provide information about problems with parents and students.
17	Ineffective assistant	To improve the assistant's classroom management.	To reassign the assistant temporarily.	To observe, document, and discuss.
18	Disabled teacher	To monitor the teacher's teaching and physical condition.	To inform the teacher about the need to terminate her teaching.	None.

TABLE 4.7 Decisions Made by Middle School Principals

#	Case	Decision about problem	Decision about solution	Decision about monitoring
5	Accelerated learning	To increase academic quality as well as diversity.	To enroll the only number of students that is possible.	To examine student achievement on a continuous basis.
6	Overloaded detention hall	To develop specific criteria for student behavior and detention. To empower teachers through alternatives.	To use the revised rules for detention and communicate them to faculty and students. To use the newly developed rules for tardiness and other nondisruptive offenses.	To review quarterly number of detentions, reasons for referral to detention, and number of detentions per teacher.
19	Students march	To keep students on campus and redirect their anger into a positive format.	To hold a rally in the auditorium and invite guest speakers.	To check student participation in the rally.
20	Excessive student misbehavior	To improve the situation regarding tardiness, absenteeism, vandalism, lack of respect, discipline, and low academic achievement.	To implement an overall program practiced in another school district.	To review all pertinent records.

21	A student's unacceptable behavior	To keep the student from disrupting classes and activities in school.	To use the school behavior system and apply it in this case.	To use the school behavior monitoring system and apply it in this case.
22	Noncompliance with a bilingual plan	To improve bilingual staffing.	To consolidate coordination responsibilities. To hire additional bilingual teachers.	To develop an administrative team's monitoring responsibilities including interaction with district personnel.

TABLE 4.8 Decisions Made by Assistant High School Principals

#	Case	Decision about problem	Decision about solution	Decision about monitoring
7	Interracial physical violence	To reduce the incidence of violence.	To form a leadership class who will communicate with gang members.	To review the information that is exchanged between members of gangs and members of the leadership class.
8	Needed grant for restructuring	To improve test scores, college enrollment rates, absenteeism and transiency.	To restructure governance, curriculum, and instruction.	To develop monitoring responsibilities for school-based management council including those related to evaluation instrumentation and consultants.
23	Needed cuts	To correct the student ratio in social studies, bilingual, and physical education classes.	To cut nine classes and two substitute teachers.	To check schedule changes. To inform all involved about reasons for the changes.
24	Attendance policy is resisted	To change attendance policy while maintaining attendance.	To implement new attendance policy.	To examine number of absences, per pupil absences, and absentees who have a passing grade.
25	A disabled student	To get the student's records. To plan for the student courses and classes. To determine needed assistance.	To enroll the student in specific classes. To assign an aide.	To develop monitoring responsibilities for the special education coordinators including interaction with the assistant principal.
26	Class overload	To work with the teachers' union about class size.	To plan solutions. To wait 30 days before selecting one; either the teacher will sign off or students will be moved.	None.

TABLE 4.9 Decisions Made by High School Principals

#	Case	Decision about problem	Decision about solution	Decision about monitoring
9	A suspension and racial discrimination charges	To reduce student aggression. To investigate charges of racial discrimination.	To meet with appropriate staff who would work with the student. To justify the fairness of the suspension decision.	To develop monitoring responsibilities by staff including observation and documentation pertinent to the student behavior.
10	Teacher is beaten in a student fight	To act decisively and with a message to the entire school community.	To promptly expel the student who struck the teacher and suspend the one who did not.	None.
27	Facing negative publicity	To develop a student forum to convey the importance of cautions about what is said to the media. To improve security.	To conduct meetings in which guidance is provided about discussions with the media. To expand the security force.	None.
28	Absence of leadership	To improve staff apathy about reporting student misbehavior. To improve rule enforcement.	To initiate discussions with staff on a regular basis. To apply the school rules in strict and ongoing ways.	To receive input from teachers and parents about attendance and punctuality and examine it.
29	A suspension and a complaint	To back the authority of the assistant principal. To handle the complaint.	To support the suspension decision. To justify the suspension decision.	None.
30	Interference with staff development	To continue with staff development plans.	To encourage teachers to continue. To raise private funds.	To gather feedback information from teachers and others involved.

proceeded with only a minimum of information. Engagement in evaluation was not extensive. In two specific cases, information was simply missing. Elementary school principals #12 and #4 (Table 4.6) had to "wait and see" because they did not have final enrollment figures for the following year. Principal #12 wanted also to secure an additional teaching position to avoid creating a combination class. Whereas each of the two principals was negotiating with the superintendent, principal #12 was creating a few combination classes and principal #4 was not creating even one such class. Principal #12 indicated to the interviewer that her real problem was combination classes. Principal #4 revealed that she was mostly concerned with having the school itself empowered to make decisions about the number of teaching positions it has. Administrative evaluation recorded in these two cases revealed that the complexity and ambiguity primarily involved information that was needed but not collected.

Whether in reality consistency and clarity of interdecisional relationships are indeed a function of only information is doubtful. Administrative use of evaluation also includes the judging of the merit of the information, an act that probably affects interdecisional relations as well. After all, a decision is typically based on the value and significance that the administrator attaches to the information at hand. Examples of this occurred in the following cases. In case #7 of the middle school principals group (Table 4.7), decisions were made on the basis of judging the information about parental pressure for accelerated learning. The result was that a parallel system of accelerated learning was developed and put in place in the school. In case #8 of the assistant high school principals group (Table 4.8), a central decision was made after judging the information about interest group pressure. Writing a grant for restructuring became a very high priority in the school. In case #30 of the high school principals group (Table 4.9), no decisions had been made at all because of an unclear judgment about the information that existed about interference with staff development. From all of the preceding cases there is reason to conclude that administrative use of evaluation that includes the collection of information and the judgment of its worth has much to do with the clarity and consistency of relationships among decisions that occur during a problem-solving process.

Additional Considerations
About Administrative Use
of Evaluation Methodologies

The question in the interviews that elicited reports of engagement in specific evaluation methodologies was: "How did you look at it?" The *it* was the evaluation object, of which there were 22 in each of the 30 interview protocols. In theory, there could have been 660 pieces of data about evaluation methodologies reported to have been used. In reality, there were fewer reported because some administrators did not look at some objects.

In relation to findings about methodologies, the per administrator number of methodologies reported to have been used was 27 for elementary school principals, 31 for high school principals, 37 for middle school principals, and 39 for assistant high school principals. In all cases, there was more than the possible one-methodology-per-administrative-evaluation-item recorded in the interview protocol. Another finding was that the use of three methodologies dominate: considering on one's own (CO), discussing in group meetings (DG), and discussing with individuals (DI). (The author acknowledges that these three methodologies are somewhat ambiguous and subjective; further refinement in future research is desirable.) The combined frequencies of CO, DG, and DI were 87.0% for elementary school principals, 87.6% for middle school principals, 91.4% for high school principals, and 93.3% for assistant high school principals.

What exactly determines the use of one evaluation methodology over another is not known. Determinants may include the following:

1. the specific problematic situation;
2. the specific situation-related decisions (A, B, C, D in the interview protocol);
3. the specific level of the school involved (elementary, middle, high school);
4. the specific size of the school (by number of students and/or staff members);
5. the specific location of the school (urban, suburban, rural);
6. the specific people in the school (who exactly is involved with the problematic situation);

7. the specific administrative help available to the administrator (assistants, colleagues, superiors);
8. the specific length and nature of the administrator's administrative experience;
9. the specific leadership style of the administrator; and
10. the specific evaluation object that the administrator looks at.

Table 4.10 depicts the frequencies of the reported use of each methodology by all administrators together in relation to each of the 22 evaluation objects.

Table 4.10 shows several interesting findings. First, it reveals again that considering on one's own (CO), discussing in group meetings (DG), and discussing with individuals (DI) are the dominant evaluation methodologies. Substantively, all of these three include the component of judging the worth of the information. DG and DI also involve collecting the information. Other methodologies mentioned in Table 4.10 could be viewed as a large part of any of the main three. Drawing on memory and experience, for example, involves information that is later judged in CO. Likewise, observing, listening, asking, and looking for are associated with DG and DI in the same way.

Frequencies of the evaluation methodologies vary by evaluation object. Sixty-six methodologies, for example, are attached to object #A.1, the problematic issues. Two other objects with a large number of methodologies are #B.1 (possible solutions) with 55, and #C.1 (solution implementation process) with 53. In the interview protocol these three evaluation objects were preceded, respectively, by decision A, the problematic situation; decision B, the problem to work on; and decision C, the solution. In each case the decision-evaluation linkage is tight in that the decision clearly stimulates engagement in evaluation. The evaluation, in turn, enhances the making of subsequent decisions in these cases. Examples in Table 4.10 of direct inputs include object #A.5 (possible specific problems to work on) with 53 methodologies inputting to decision B, the problem to work on, and object #C.4 (cost of solution implementation) with 41 methodologies inputting to decision D, monitoring.

Another object, #A.2 (origin of the issues), also had a high score: 52 methodologies. Here the methodologies are employed to study in depth the previous item, #A.1 (the problematic issues). #A.2 also

(*text continues on page 91*)

TABLE 4.10 The Use of Evaluation Objects and Evaluation Methodologies as Reported by 30 School Administrators

#	Evaluation object	Considering on one's own	Discussing with individuals	Discussion in groups	Drawing on memory/experience	Observing	Listening	Asking	Looking for	Examining document	Informing	Imposing	Total
A.1	Problematic issues	12	14	13	2	5	9	4	3	4	–	–	66
A.2	Origin of issues	13	15	11	3	–	3	3	–	4	–	–	52
A.3	Participants in issues	13	19	13	–	1	1	–	–	–	–	–	47
A.4	Those responsible for issues	15	17	11	1	–	–	–	–	1	–	–	45
A.5	Possible specific problems to work on	17	20	14	2	–	–	–	–	–	–	–	53
A.6	Owners of possible problems	19	15	11	1	–	–	–	–	–	1	–	47

(continued)

TABLE 4.10 Continued

#	Evaluation object	Considering on one's own	Discussing with individuals	Discussion in groups	Drawing on memory/exper.	Observing	Listening	Asking	Looking for	Examining document	Informing	Imposing	Total
							Evaluation methodologies						
A.7	Priorities of problem owners	20	11	11	1	1	–	1	–	1	1	–	47
A.8	Possible effects of problems	16	12	12	–	–	2	1	2	1	–	–	46
A.9	Predicted manageability of problems	19	12	7	1	–	1	–	–	–	–	–	40
B.1	Possible solutions of the chosen problems to work on	12	16	19	1	–	1	3	–	3	1	–	55
B.2	Owners of possible solutions	15	14	17	–	–	–	–	–	–	–	–	46

B.3	Priorities of solution owners	13	14	16	–	–	–	1	–	–	–	2	46
B.4	Possible effects of solution	17	13	14	1	1	1	1	1	–	–	–	49
B.5	Cost of solutions	18	10	10	1	–	–	2	1	–	–	–	52
B.6	Predicted manageability of solutions	20	14	10	1	–	–	–	–	–	–	–	45
C.1	Solution implementation process	8	12	17	1	1	3	2	–	1	2	1	53
C.2	Possible effectiveness of the solution implementation process	18	12	11	1	1	–	1	–	–	–	–	43
C.3	Predicted manageability of the solution implementation process	21	9	5	2	1	–	2	–	–	–	–	43
C.4	Cost of solution implementation process	19	9	10	1	–	1	1	–	–	–	–	41

(continued)

TABLE 4.10 Continued

#	Evaluation object	Evaluation methodologies											
		Considering on one's own	Discussing with individuals	Discussion in groups	Drawing on memory/exper.	Observing	Listening	Asking	Looking for	Examining document	Informing	Imposing	Total
C.5	Owners of solution implementation process	21	10	11	–	–	–	–	1	–	–	–	43
D.1	Cost of design of monitoring solution implementation	11	9	10	1	–	1	1	1	–	–	–	34
D.2	Possible effectiveness of design of monitoring solution implementation	13	8	9	2	–	1	1	1	–	–	–	35

shows four instances of the methodology of examining documents. Some issues require it. Some administrators insist on it.

Other data may be of interest. The school administrators identified people (actors) in five evaluation instances. The evaluation objects and the corresponding number of methodologies reported are as follows:

1. #A.3 (participants in the issues): 45
2. #A.4 (those responsible for the issues): 43
3. #A.6 (owners of possible problems): 47
4. #B.2 (owners of possible solutions): 46
5. #C.5 (owners of possible solution implementation process): 43

Several administrators were found to report the exact same evaluation methodologies in all five or at least four of these items. If replicated, this finding may imply that each administrator has his or her own way of finding information about people and judging it during a problem-solving process, regardless of where in the process the administrator happens to be.

Summary

This chapter has offered syntheses of some of the findings that were derived from the reports of 30 school administrators in personal interviews. Evaluation practice patterns emerged in association with the problematic situations and the key decisions.

All 30 administrators reported to have faced and observed the problematic situation. They mentioned difficulties in doing so, but none reported that the risks of facing the situation outweighed the benefits of doing so. Many talked about the high cost of ignoring it. As to observing the situation, all 30 administrators reported to have been heavily involved in evaluation throughout the entire problem-solving process.

Several of the 30 administrators also attempted to specify and describe the situation. Some reported that such actions enhanced their control of the situation and minimized their feeling of discomfort with it. They did it with the aid of evaluation. An elementary school principal said about decision B, for example: "The problem to work on is not readily known or agreed upon in the early stages, but it clears up after you evaluate the issues." A high school principal said about evaluation #A.1: "Describing the issues tells you the scope of the problematic situation."

As to the four key decisions, three fourths of the administrators found it prudent to make all four of them (problematic situation, problems to work on, solution, monitoring). One fourth made only the first three decisions. In cases where decisions were also clarified, there was consistency among them. In cases where decisions were not clarified, the relationship among them was complex and ambiguous. Administrative use of evaluation and information gathering in particular enhanced consistency and clarity. One assistant high school principal said the following about consistency and clarity: "It is impossible to become consistent without information. It is impossible to remain consistent without informing everyone involved."

This chapter ended with added considerations of the use of administrative evaluations—those that occur alongside administrative decisions in problematic situations. The data in this book confirm that school administrators engage in evaluations, and that they also use them to make decisions. Engaging implies determining what objects to evaluate, what evaluation methodologies to employ, and what kinds of findings to derive. Engaging also means conducting all the above activities in accord with a specific evaluation purpose. Three evaluation methodologies were used frequently in schools: considering on one's own, discussing with groups, and discussing with individuals.

In this study the use of evaluations in and for making decisions implies weighing the evaluation findings and incorporating them into subsequent decisions. The number of evaluation findings was a function of the particular evaluation object. Objects that were looked at immediately *following* a decision produced multiple evaluation findings. Objects that were looked at immediately *preceding* a subsequent decision (such as effectiveness, cost, manageability) produced only a few findings. It is possible that early engagement in evaluation makes the involvement in problematic situations easier.

The following guidelines are offered to practicing school administrators:

1. Face, observe, and (with the help of evaluation) specify and describe problematic situations in school when you see them.
2. Make key decisions as part of the problem-solving process and clarify these decisions to all concerned.
3. In accord with needed decisions and selected purposes, choose evaluation objects, employ appropriate methodologies to evaluate them, derive corresponding evaluation findings, and use the findings as input to subsequent decisions in your problem-solving process.

5

HOW THE CASES INFORM THEORY

Evaluation in Administration

This chapter takes up conceptual issues. One group of issues focuses on characteristics of administrative use of evaluation itself. The other group deals with the relationship between evaluation and decisions in administration.

The research described in this book acquaints the reader with what administrative use of evaluation actually is. This is the kind of evaluation that is performed by school administrators rather than by professional evaluators. It is the kind of evaluation that is performed in the context of major decision steps (e.g., Gorton & Snowden, 1993), particularly if the steps are viewed as taking place within a decision-making process rather than in connection with a major terminal administrative decision. The latter would typically require a professionally run evaluation project or at the least a professional evaluation. An example might be a revamping of the entire school curriculum.

The technique utilized in this research has been a simple and fundamental fact-finding procedure. A structure of decisions was adapted from the literature on administrative decision making. A structure of evaluations was adapted from the literature on educational evaluation. I hypothesized that a joint structure was operating in problematic situations that administrators face in schools. The joint structure was tested for its appropriateness in practical situations in schools and used to gather information about what school administrators report has occurred in actual situations.

Information was gathered from 30 school administrators in Southern California as responses to the interview protocol. Summaries of the 30 cases, including the 22 instances of administrative use of evaluation in each case, were presented earlier in this book, as were some specific findings at the aggregate level. No one should expect these findings to change schools directly. But the more school administrators understand that administrative use of evaluation is under their total control, the more they may realize the "facilitative power" they gain when they engage in such evaluation. The connection between facilitative power and school site management and school restructuring has already been examined recently (e.g., Goldman, Dunlap, & Conley, 1993).

It may be that the findings in the study reported in this book could change schools only as a result of theoretical scrutiny (e.g., Travers, 1983). To this end, further research has to include questions such as: What else has to be done to prove that administrative use of evaluation exists? What important characteristics does it have? Under which conditions does it occur? What impact does it have on administrative decisions and problem solving?

As with most other social-scientific endeavors, the research effort described in this book has generated modest theoretical expectations. Its conceptual objectives have been (a) to somehow shake up some myths about administrative use of evaluation and (b) to serve as a tool for new conceptual configurations (e.g., Young, 1983). In particular, the findings create serious doubts about the absence of evaluation as a major and central dimension of the practice of school administration. The findings also seriously question the notion that this evaluation cannot be easily investigated. Not only are these two myths without foundation, but this study shows that in several instances the very practice of evaluation enhances administrative efficiency and effectiveness.

Decision-Making
Process
Evaluations — Decisions

Figure 5.1. Decision Making X (e.g., Stufflebeam, 1971; Glasman, 1986a, 1986b; Simon & Associates, 1986; Glasman & Nevo, 1988).

Decision-Evaluation Relationships

Perhaps nothing will better help destroy the myth that school administrators do not evaluate than the proved fact that administrative decisions and administrative use of evaluations are actually linked together. The issue was examined extensively during the 1980s. At that time, the relationship between administrative decisions and administrative use of evaluations was conceived as it is portrayed in Figure 5.1. Evaluations served as inputs to decisions and all were in the context of a decision-making process. This was accepted as given when evaluations were organized as management tools (e.g., Barry, Alkin, & Ruskus, 1985) where professional evaluators do the evaluations and where the concern was that evaluation results would indeed be utilized by decision makers (e.g., Sirotnik, 1987).

The research reported in this book focuses on evaluations in which administrators engage, rather than those in which evaluators engage. It also discusses conditions of a problematic situation in which the ingredients of the decision-making process are magnified and shown in multiple units. In this relationship, there are four step-decisions and 22 evaluations. The step-decisions are, respectively, about the problematic situation, the problem to work on, the solution and its implementation, and the monitoring of the solution implementation. The evaluations are about issues, participants, and other considerations. Figure 5.2 portrays this situation.

There is ample conceptual and empirical justification for the existence of elements that are common to both administrative decisions and evaluations. Simon (1961) suggested that rationality exists in the origin of decisions and of evaluations. Simon also proposed that decisions and evaluations may share a common form. This book

Decision Making

DECISION A

Evaluation 1
Evaluation 2
Evaluation 3
Evaluation 4
Evaluation 5
Evaluation 6
Evaluation 7
Evaluation 8
Evaluation 9

DECISION B

Evaluation 1
Evaluation 2
Evaluation 3
Evaluation 4
Evaluation 5
Evaluation 6

DECISION C

Evaluation 1
Evaluation 2
Evaluation 3
Evaluation 4
Evaluation 5

DECISION D

Evaluation 1
Evaluation 2

Figure 5.2. Decision Making Y

reports that similar components have been found in decisions and in evaluations. It is possible that administrative decisions and evaluations are interdependent in that some evaluation components are also components of some decisions. This happens primarily with evaluations that immediately precede decisions and with those that immediately follow them.

In discussing the planning activities that occur early in the decision-making process, Simon and Associates (1986) identified fixing agendas, setting goals, and designing actions as the major elements. The research in this book has ignored evaluation-decision linkages in planning activities. These activities are commonly found under regular and calm conditions more than in problematic situations in which the administrator often does not have much time to engage in extensive planning. Chapter 4 suggests that the administrator face the problematic situation, observe it, specify it, and describe it. Much research would be needed to better understand how administrative use of evaluations and administrative decisions link in conditions of problematic situations. Conceptually, other questions are also of interest: How does one prove that the administrative decision-evaluation linkage exists very early in the problem-solving process? What characteristics does it have? Under what conditions? What impact does it have on later stages of the linkages?

What Next?

The study of administrative use of evaluation began with the early conceptions of evaluations as specific administrative tasks such as teacher evaluation and curriculum evaluation. It has progressed to the employment of information and judgments in connection with decisions associated with a problematic situation. A recently developed and accepted assumption has been that administrators evaluate almost all the time and not only when their task is an evaluation task.

It is difficult to study administrative use of evaluation when the need for evaluation in practice is not great. This book produced findings about evaluation under conditions when the need is great—problematic situations. The instrument used here helped identify ingredients of the process of administrative use of evaluation. Given the array of 30 cases presented here, the interview protocol proved useful in describing the exercise of evaluation by school administrators when they deal with the district office and with their staffs in the school.

It is quite possible that major changes currently occurring in the schools will require a more intensive practice of administrative use of evaluation. Under such conditions it would be extremely useful to study evaluation as it enhances school empowerment and shared decision making. After all, site management implies increased decision making and, therefore, also increased administrative use of evaluation.

Administrative use of evaluation needs to be studied as a political mechanism, too. Evaluation interacts with political values to form changes just as it interacts with pedagogic and administrative values to bring about stability. Political dimensions exist when a problematic situation arises. They continue to be present until all of the monitoring devices are in place at the end of the problem-solving processes.

A final observation is in order. Administrative use of evaluation may lend itself to extremely rigorous scientific conditions only to a limit. Indeed, the model (Chapter 2) was adapted from some dimensions of systematic evaluation (Chapter 1). Also, most quotes from Simon could apply only to rational choice-based decisions. The truth is, however, that a large variation was found in this study in terms of degrees of rationality and systemization in the practice of evaluation. Surely, habit, regard for others, moral values, ethical values, and emotions (e.g., Zey, 1992) also dictate what happens when school administrators evaluate. Most of the time their decisions are reasoned choices. Their evaluations help them make their choices more effectively (Chapter 1).

6

PRACTICAL APPLICATIONS
OF THE EVALUATION INSTRUMENT

Introduction

This chapter focuses again on the instrument that has been developed in this book. Until now in this book, the instrument's utility has been limited to that of a protocol in interviews with school administrators about their problematic situations. This chapter demonstrates the instrument's use in two additional ways. One is for principals' self-assessment. The other is for the evaluation of the principal by his or her superordinate, typically the district's assistant superintendent for instruction.

This chapter is not a prescription for a principal evaluation system (e.g., Abbott, 1974; Hunt & Buser, 1977; Bolton, 1980; Glasman, 1986a). Rather, it is a conceptually backed and research-derived set of applications for use by administrators as they see fit. The applications have clear purposes—self-assessment and evaluation by the supervisor—all for improvement and change (e.g., Castetter, 1976; Fawcett, 1979; Webb, Greer, Montello, & Norton, 1987; Deal, Neufeld, & Rallis, 1982; Duke & Stiggens, 1985; Murphy, Hallinger, Peterson, & Lotto, 1987; Glasman & Heck, 1992-1993).

Fundamentally, the following was done for the purpose of this chapter. One elementary school principal in Goleta, California, was asked to study the instrument and use it to record his thoughts and actions for two consecutive days with regard to the problematic situations that he faced during this period of time. More specifically, the principal was asked to do the recording by the instrument's four decisions and 22 sets of evaluations for every problematic situation he encountered. After the end of the two-day period, the principal was interviewed about his recordings. Following that, the principal's superordinate was shown the recording that the principal prepared and she was interviewed about it. The primary objective of the two interviews was to assess the two individuals' reactions to the possibility that the recorded information might serve for the principal's self-assessment and for the superordinate's evaluation of the principal.

Recording Ongoing Thoughts and Actions

Mr. Daniel Cooperman, the principal of Isla Vista School in Goleta, California, agreed to record his thoughts and activities by problematic situations, decisions, and evaluations. He saw himself as the most likely logger if the information was to be gathered about his work—better than someone else observing and shadowing him. Isla Vista School enrolls 675 students on two campuses. Sixty-eight percent of the students are limited-English-proficient pupils. The school is one of eight in this elementary district. Mr. Cooperman has administered the school for 3 years. He has one assistant principal in a half-time capacity.

The actual recording took place on February 16th and 17th, 1993 —five days after Mr. Cooperman was asked to do so. He actually encountered three problematic situations during the 2-day period. The first problematic situation involved an itinerant employee. Mr. Cooperman began dealing with this situation at 11:00 a.m. on Tuesday and ended at 3:00 p.m. the same day. He recorded the situation in parts: at noon, at 2:00 p.m., and at 4:00 p.m. on the same day. The second problematic situation involved the curriculum. It had been worked on since November of 1992. Mr. Cooperman dealt with this situation from Tuesday at 3:00 p.m. until Wednesday at 10:00 a.m. The recording was done at 6:00 p.m. on Tuesday and at 10:00 a.m. on Wednesday. Mr. Cooperman did not record the third problematic situation he encountered. When asked why later, he said that it was too complex and he did not have the time to sort it out. In Figures 6.1 and 6.2 are the recordings of the two cases that he did record.

The Use of the Information
for Self-Assessment

Much use of self-assessment has been tried in teaching (e.g., Barber, 1990). Teachers have used self-assessment as a framework for self-improvement and also for initiating changes in their methods and techniques. In self-assessment, teachers have used video and audiotape feedback, self-rating forms, self-reports, and a variety of techniques in which another person observes them. There have also been instances of self-assessment based on teachers' own recording of their actions.

Much less self-assessment has been practiced in administration (e.g., Glasman & Heck, 1992-1993). Overall attention to principal assessment has not been as strong as the attention paid to evaluating teaching. The reasons are many. Principals are not in the classrooms. They also move around a lot. Principals do not have lesson plans as teachers do. Their work is more unpredictable. It has been difficult to videotape and shadow principals as a means of recording their actions. Principals themselves have not employed many new ways of self-assessment regardless of the means of collecting information.

The instrument developed in this book can be used for principal self-assessment. In such a case, the principal would record his or her activities by a problematic situation, decisions, and evaluations, then examine what has been recorded and (it is hoped) learn from it. Because Mr. Cooperman had already recorded two problematic situations he had faced in 2 days I decided to seek his opinion on the use of the data he collected for self-assessment. An edited version of the interview with Mr. Cooperman that took place on February 24, 1993, begins on page 115. The interview dealt with these issues.

(text continues on page 115)

Figure 6.1. Case #1: An Itinerant Employee (pages 103-108)

BACKGROUND INFORMATION: Grade levels in school K-6 Number of students in school 675

Years you have been in the present job 3 Number of administrators in the school 2
DESCRIBE A PROBLEMATIC SITUATION YOU FACED RECENTLY:

An itinerant employee of the district was transferred to the school to serve as an aide to the speech therapist. As the school principal perceives it, coordination for the move was complicated by the lack of communication between different departments within the district, including the district personnel administrator, district special education administrator, site principal, site vice-principal, teachers affected by the transfer, and staff person affected by the transfer. The speech therapist complained about the aide's lack of sufficient training. The complaint occurred on Tuesday, February 16, 1993, at 11:00 a.m.

TIME: Tuesday and Wednesday, February 16 and 17, 1993

_____

_____

_____

_____

_____

_____

_____

_____

(continued)

A. DID YOU DECIDE TO OBSERVE AND PARTICIPATE IN THE PROBLEMATIC SITUATION? <u>Yes</u>

WHAT DID YOU LOOK FOR?	HOW DID YOU LOOK AT IT?	WHAT DID YOU FIND OUT?
THE PROBLEMATIC ISSUES	Discussing with individuals	1. Lack of communication between the district's personnel director and the principal 2. Speech therapist would have liked to have been consulted 3. Aide lacks in training
THE ORIGIN OF THE ISSUES	Considering on his own	1. Desire on the part of the district to transfer individual to a higher paying position
THE PARTICIPANTS IN THE ISSUES	Considering on his own	1. Principal, vice-principal, aide, speech therapist, special education teacher, district personnel director, district special education director
THOSE RESPONSIBLE FOR THE ISSUES	Considering on his own	1. All of the above
POSSIBLE SPECIFIC PROBLEMS TO WORK ON	Considering on his own Discussing with others	1. Lack of communication at district and at school level 2. Overreaction of speech therapist
THE OWNERS OF POSSIBLE PROBLEMS	Considering on his own	1. Speech therapist
THE PRIORITIES OF PROBLEM OWNERS	Considering on his own	1. Needs help badly—speaks only English

104

| THE POSSIBLE EFFECTS OF THE PROBLEMS | Discussing with individuals | 1. Low morale |
| THE PREDICTED MANAGEABILITY OF THE PROBLEMS | Considering on his own | 1. The situation will calm down; it is a matter of time |

(continued)

B. DID YOU DECIDE ON A PROBLEM TO WORK ON? Yes IF SO, WHAT WAS THE PROBLEM? Communication improvement and information acquisition for the benefit of school people.

WHAT DID YOU LOOK FOR?	HOW DID YOU LOOK AT IT?	WHAT DID YOU FIND OUT?
THE POSSIBLE SOLUTIONS OF THE PROBLEM CHOSEN TO WORK ON	Discussing with a group	1. Aide would work with special education teacher 2. Aide could acquire additional training elsewhere 3. Problem owners exchange information
THE OWNERS OF THE POSSIBLE SOLUTIONS	Considering on his own	1. Aide 2 Speech therapist 3. Special education teacher
THE PRIORITIES OF SOLUTION	Considering on his own	1. Pay raise, stability 2. Help 3. Help
THE POSSIBLE EFFECTS OF THE SOLUTIONS	Considering on his own	1. Improve morale
THE COST OF THE SOLUTIONS	Considering on his own Discussing with individuals	1. Everybody's time 2. Two hours of principal's time
THE MANAGEABILITY OF THE SOLUTIONS	Considering on his own	1. Hopeful

C. DID YOU DECIDE ON A SOLUTION AND DID YOU IMPLEMENT IT? Yes __ IF SO, WHAT WAS THE SOLUTION? To assign the aide to the special education teacher for one week and to postpone the continuation of the speech therapy for one week. Subsequently, when the transfer occurs, to hire another aide for special education.

WHAT DID YOU LOOK FOR?	HOW DID YOU LOOK AT IT?	WHAT DID YOU FIND OUT?
THE SOLUTION IMPLEMENTATION PROCESS	Discussing with a group	1. Clear and manageable 2. Need to teach aide about her role in speech therapy
THE POSSIBLE EFFECTIVENESS OF THE SOLUTION IMPLEMENTATION PROCESS	Considering on his own	1. Strongly positive
THE PREDICTED MANAGEABILITY OF THE SOLUTION IMPLEMENTATION PROCESS	Considering on his own	1. Hopeful
THE COST OF THE SOLUTION IMPLEMENTATION PROCESS	Considering on his own	1. Solution may not be the best, but it is a good one and it has three committed owners
THE OWNERS OF THE SOLUTION IMPLEMENTATION PROCESS	Considering on his own	1. The aide 2. The special education teacher 3. The speech therapist

(continued)

D. DID YOU DECIDE ON A DESIGN FOR A MONITORING SOLUTION IMPLEMENTATION AND DID YOU IMPLEMENT IT? Yes, <u>yes</u> IF SO, WHAT WAS THE DESIGN? Periodic informal checks on aide's work. Additional informal checks on solution with school district office.

WHAT DID YOU LOOK FOR?	HOW LONG DID YOU LOOK AT IT?	WHAT DID YOU FIND OUT?
THE COST OF THE DESIGN FOR A MONITORING SOLUTION IMPLEMENTATION	Considering on his own	1. Time, but minimal
THE POSSIBLE EFFECTIVENESS OF THE DESIGN FOR A MONITORING SOLUTION IMPLEMENTATION	Considering on his own	1. Hopeful if principal's time permits (a) a continuation of enhancing the ownership of the three parties in making the transfer effective, and (b) enhancing a coordination of communication in the district office

Figure 6.2. Case #2: The Curriculum (pages 109-114)

BACKGROUND INFORMATION: Grade levels in school K-6 Number of students in school 675

Years you have been in the present job 3 Number of administrators in the school 2

DESCRIBE A PROBLEMATIC SITUATION YOU FACED RECENTLY:

A schoolwide academic downturn has been occurring for close to 2 years. A decision was made in November of 1992 to address the downturn spiral. The major problem that emerged in relation to the downturn was the lack of long-term effective goals in the curriculum domain. Much previous effort was to culminate on Tuesday when the principal would present the goals to the site council at its evening meeting. While the attempt to tackle the downturn has been a continuous one, every person concerned saw the presentation of the goals by the principal to the board as a pivotal move. The new objectives would cover four areas as follows: (a) create a program for schoolwide involvement of parents; (b) clarify behaviors and learning expectations for each child; (c) expand opportunities for teachers to share ideas and information in professional development; and (d) increase levels of self-respect and self-esteem on the part of children and adults.

TIME: Tuesday and Wednesday, February 16 and 17, 1993

(continued)

109

A. DID YOU DECIDE TO OBSERVE AND PARTICIPATE IN THE PROBLEMATIC SITUATION? <u>Yes</u>

WHAT DID YOU LOOK FOR?	HOW DID YOU LOOK AT IT?	WHAT DID YOU FIND OUT?
THE PROBLEMATIC ISSUES	Discussing with groups Discussing with individuals	1. Found general agreement in school about objectives 2. Not completely clear about presentation to council
THE ORIGIN OF THE ISSUES	Considering on his own	1. Need to increase student achievement 2. Need to improve discipline 3. Need to enhance growth
THE PARTICIPANTS IN THE ISSUES	Discussing with groups Discussing with individuals	1. Principal 2. Teachers 3. Parents 4. Students
THOSE RESPONSIBLE FOR THE ISSUES	Discussing with groups Discussing with individuals	1. As above
POSSIBLE SPECIFIC PROBLEMS TO WORK ON	Considering on his own	1. Enhance council's motivation to lead in the effort
THE OWNERS OF POSSIBLE PROBLEMS	Considering on his own	1. As in "participants" and "responsible" above
THE PRIORITIES OF PROBLEM OWNERS	Considering on his own	1. For all, ease and convenience of changes

THE POSSIBLE EFFECTS OF THE PROBLEMS	Considering on his own	1. Unknown yet
THE PREDICTED MANAGEABILITY OF THE PROBLEMS	Considering on his own	1. Hopeful but unknown

(continued)

B. DID YOU DECIDE ON A PROBLEM TO WORK ON? Yes IF SO, WHAT WAS THE PROBLEM? Consider the four major goals that the site council approved the night before as guidelines for the school plan that now needs to be prepared.

WHAT DID YOU LOOK FOR?	HOW DID YOU LOOK AT IT?	WHAT DID YOU FIND OUT?
THE POSSIBLE SOLUTIONS OF THE PROBLEM CHOSEN TO WORK ON	Discussing with groups	1. School staff under the leadership of the two administrators will begin to work on the school plan elsewhere
THE OWNERS OF THE POSSIBLE SOLUTIONS	Discussing with groups	1. Administrators 2. Teachers
THE PRIORITIES OF SOLUTION	Discussing with groups	1. High priorities
THE POSSIBLE EFFECTS OF THE SOLUTIONS	Discussing with groups	1. Improve morale
THE COST OF THE SOLUTIONS	Discussing with groups	1. Time
THE MANAGEABILITY OF THE SOLUTIONS	Discussing with groups	1. Should be easy to manage

112

C. DID YOU DECIDE ON A SOLUTION AND DID YOU IMPLEMENT IT? Yes IF SO, WHAT WAS THE SOLUTION? The solution about the school plan has not yet been implemented.

WHAT DID YOU LOOK FOR?	HOW DID YOU LOOK AT IT?	WHAT DID YOU FIND OUT?
THE SOLUTION IMPLEMENTATION PROCESS	Considering on his own	1. It is forthcoming
THE POSSIBLE EFFECTIVENESS OF THE SOLUTION IMPLEMENTATION PROCESS	Considering on his own	1. Could be highly effective
THE PREDICTED MANAGEABILITY OF THE SOLUTION IMPLEMENTATION PROCESS	Considering on his own	1. Unclear
THE COST OF THE SOLUTION IMPLEMENTATION PROCESS	Considering on his own	1. Time
THE OWNERS OF THE SOLUTION IMPLEMENTATION PROCESS	Considering on his own	1. Administrators 2. Staff

(continued)

D. DID YOU DECIDE ON A DESIGN FOR A MONITORING SOLUTION IMPLEMENTATION AND DID YOU IMPLEMENT IT? Yes IF SO, WHAT WAS THE DESIGN? <u>Site council will evaluate the plan.</u>

WHAT DID YOU LOOK FOR?	HOW LONG DID YOU LOOK AT IT?	WHAT DID YOU FIND OUT?
THE COST OF THE DESIGN FOR A MONITORING SOLUTION IMPLEMENTATION	Considering on his own	1. Meeting time
THE POSSIBLE EFFECTIVENESS OF THE DESIGN FOR A MONITORING SOLUTION IMPLEMENTATION	Considering on his own	1. Uncertain at this time

114

Glasman: Was it a problem for you to record two problematic situations?

Cooperman: Not at all.

Glasman: Was the order of the items in the instrument a problem?

Cooperman: The order was great. In most cases it matched the order of what really happened, but not always.

Glasman: What was the most difficult problem you encountered in recording?

Cooperman: I recorded Case #1 in three sittings and Case #2 in two. I chose to do it this way. My problem was that very often I wanted to go into more depth, but I did not have the time.

Glasman: So what was the problem?

Cooperman: Containing myself. The evaluation items were very stimulating.

Glasman: What did you miss when you avoided going into depth?

Cooperman: Analysis. Real self-evaluation. I plan to do it in a couple of weekends.

Glasman: What have you already seen *about* Case #1?

Cooperman: It is a medium-range problematic situation—4 hours or so. To differentiate evaluation from decisions is difficult here sometimes. It is easier in a long-range problematic situation like Case #2.

Glasman: Is it because in short- or medium-range problematic situations evaluation and decisions do not proceed necessarily in the order suggested by the instrument?

Cooperman: Not necessarily. My mind in general does not easily differentiate between decisions and evaluations because a lot of evaluations require interim decisions like what to look at, what to record, and so forth. I guess it has to do with time. Give me more time and I can learn to differentiate more easily. By the way, I love the order of the evaluations between decision A and decision B. The problematic situation simply became more specific as you went down the list of these nine evaluations.

Glasman: What about your evaluation methodologies?

Cooperman: In the personnel case I used primarily considering on one's own (CO) and discussing with individuals (DI). I had to.

Everything occurred fast. I had no time for group meetings. In the curricula case I used primarily discussing in groups (DG). Everyone needs to get involved here. By the way, DG was heavy in Case #1 in the first evaluations after decisions B and C, respectively. I wondered why do we need DG so early in the process?

Glasman: Can I ask you a "funny" question?

Cooperman: Sure.

Glasman: How come the number of owners decreases between the first and ninth evaluation in Case #1?

Cooperman: Do you really think that to talk about a problem is the same as to be responsible for it?

Glasman: I also noticed that the evaluations after decisions C and D, respectively, in Case #2, are only speculative.

Cooperman: The case is still ongoing.

Glasman: Have you already completed the self-assessment in these two days?

Cooperman: Almost, in Case #2. No, in Case #1. Let me explain. In Case #1 I concluded by convincing myself that I do not have to own every problem, so long as the solution is within policy. I had believed differently in the past. I no longer do. Now I am convinced that I do own the evaluation I engage in. I am responsible for it and its results. In Case #2 I concluded that there is a long way to go. I still do not fully understand my role in this case.

Glasman: Is it harder to own an evaluation or a decision?

Cooperman: If you know what you are doing, evaluation is always yours; decision is yours only some of the time.

Glasman: What do *you* mean by evaluation?

Cooperman: Getting the information and judging its worth.

The Use of the Information
for Evaluation by the Superordinate

The district's assistant superintendent for instruction may also make use of the principal's self-recorded information. Much more information would be needed here in comparison to the information gathered for self-assessment. Possible durations include from

5 to 10 consecutive days, 2 days a week for 3 to 5 weeks, 2 randomly chosen days form each month, and so forth.

Some such work has been done in evaluating teaching. In cases like this a portfolio (e.g., Bird, 1990) is prepared that logs the activities. The purposes of such portfolios include improvement and conflict resolution. The portfolios include plans, assignments, tests, videotapes, transcripts, and written testimonials. Some portfolios have also been prepared in the evaluation of administrators (e.g., Glasman & Heck, 1992-1993). They include plans, videotapes, and transcripts.

What has been tried here is new. The information that Mr. Cooperman gathered about his thoughts and actions has been shared with his assistant superintendent for the purpose of evaluating his work as principal. Below is an edited version of the interview with Mrs. Ida Rickborn, the assistant superintendent for instruction in the Goleta Elementary School District. The interview took place on March 4, 1993.

Glasman: After hearing me read you Mr. Cooperman's detailed recording of the two problematic situations, how do you think the recording could be used?

Rickborn: I can react now, but I could react more usefully if I had a chance to spend a bit more time with the categories that appear in the instrument.

Glasman: Could you just say what comes to your mind now?

Rickborn: Sure. I detect a pattern of analysis, a logical structure. I can see how it would be easy for the principal to respond and for the district evaluator to understand.

Glasman: What questions could you answer about the principal using this instrument?

Rickborn: How does the principal identify issues? Are the issues clear? Has he been able to identify the major problems and how do the smaller issues contribute to the major problems? How fully is the principal aware of the participants? Areas of responsibilities? Has he chosen the best solutions? Why? I could go on. I think each evaluation category in the instrument produces valuable data for my evaluation of the principal.

Glasman: Would you use these data to also evaluate the principal in comparison with other principals?

Rickborn: Yes. For example, how do different principals handle performance conflict situations? A curriculum situation? Comparison by domains of problems is useful.

Glasman: How would you use your evaluation?

Rickborn: If I had enough data, say about 2 days per week for 6 weeks, I could generalize about each principal as to how he or she attacks problems. These data would help the principal learn the suitability of a solution to a problem. They would help me guide the principal's search for such learning. The more I do it, the more I expect the principal would develop an urge for self-analysis beyond what is required of him or her by the district.

Glasman: Which principals would benefit most?

Rickborn: The instrument could benefit every single principal in my district, but most of all those who are not thinking much in a structured way. They would find the structure in the instrument very helpful in identifying issues and articulating them.

Glasman: What does it take before the tool can be used for self-assessment and/or evaluation supervisors?

Rickborn: Nothing but practice with the tool. One needs learning time and training time. It should not take very long; a total of a day, perhaps. School districts could organize a staff development day for principals and for their evaluators. Principals could practice in school, and the supervisors could practice in their evaluation conferences with the principals.

Glasman: Do you think that this could lead to change?

Rickborn: Very definitely—change in the school building and change in the district office. Any good evaluation leads to change.

Summary

This chapter has provided one example of how the instrument developed in this book might be used by school principals and their district office evaluators. First, the instrument's use was shown in recording ongoing thoughts and actions that the principal is involved in while facing problematic situations. Next the instrument demonstrated how the principal might use this information for self-assessment and how the assistant superintendent for instruction might use the information to evaluate the principal. The chapter showed that these two sets of tasks are not only possible but also perceived as beneficial.

This chapter has also provided the cap to this book. It compliments the cap that was introduced at the start of the book. Each reflects different ways of summarizing previous research about evaluation as an administrative function. The summary gives rise to the development of an instrument. The instrument, in turn, serves as a tool for further research about evaluation in administration that is somewhat more systematic than what is typical of this field. The findings of this research stimulated the study of the use of the instrument for ongoing practical work. The cap has always been the research and systematic studies. But practice has always provided new bottles that need to be covered.

This chapter is a beginning, too. It is a start of new ways for viewing, studying, and practicing evaluation in the principalship. With the intensification of the demands of accountability, administrators are on the defensive now. They need to consider site management, empowerment, shared decision making, and several other accompanying changes. They need new ways to assume responsibilities alongside the power, ways that go beyond the common duties of personnel and program evaluation (e.g., Stufflebeam & Webster, 1988; Kowalski & Reitzug, 1993, pp. 36-37).

School administrators now need to evaluate everything—what they see, what they do, and what they are about to do. Their evaluation perspective needs to be assertive, comprehensive, and as much in depth as possible. They need to become visibly accountable without losing their effectiveness as instructional, organizational, and educational leaders. It is hoped that this book has been a helpful starting tool.

RESOURCE A
SUMMARY OF CASES #11 TO #30

Case #11 When Teachers Do Not Want Combination Classes at the School

Case #12 When the Number of Students to Be Enrolled in the School Is Uncertain

Case #13 When the Teaching Staff Disagrees About Bilingual Education's Value

Case #14 When Students' Homes Are Blamed for Student Failure in School

Case #15 When the Principal Believes That the School's Image Requires Changing

Case #16 When Parents Resent Reputedly Weak Teachers

Case #17 When a Teaching Aide Is Totally Ineffective

Case #18 When a Disabled Teacher Can No Longer Teach Effectively

Case #19 When Students Want to Demonstrate Outside of the Campus

Case #20 When Misbehavior of Students Becomes Excessive

Case #21 When the Behavior of a Student Becomes Unacceptable

Case #22 When the School Does Not Comply With a Bilingual Master Plan

Case #23 When Major Cuts Have to Be Made

Case #24 When a Student Attendance Policy Is Problematic
Case #25 When a Severely Disabled Student Enrolls in the School
Case #26 When Classes Are Overcrowded
Case #27 When a School Community Faces Negative Publicity
Case #28 When School Leadership Has Been Lacking
Case #29 When Students Are Suspended and a Mother Complains
Case #30 When There Is Interference With Implementing Staff Development Plans

CASE #11

When Teachers Do Not Want Combination Classes at the School

In this case the principal, Mr. Robert Jackson, has been administering schools for 16 years and is beginning his second year in the current school. This elementary school enrolls about 400 students. The problematic situation Mr. Jackson recalled involved instructional issues, personnel issues, student personnel issues, and budgetary issues. The problem first appeared at the beginning of 1992. The principal felt at the time that he was coming into a situation where the teaching staff had been "someone else's creation" and not his. He had noticed that some teachers in the first and second grades were in competition with each other. Two of the classes contained 20 second graders and 5 first graders each. The 10 first graders were uncomfortable. Parents complained; they wanted all the 10 first graders together.

Both combination classes were taught by veteran teachers. One agreed to use a new handwriting program and one did not. One cared about curriculum continuity in the school and one did not. One was a team player and the other was not. The latter teacher often joked with the principal about doing research in both classes, comparing results, and arriving at conclusions about the worthwhileness of the school's "questionable" innovations.

The principal decided to observe and participate in the problematic situation. He first looked at problematic issues. Initially he observed, and when he did not understand things, he began to ask questions. The answers he received provided information about the problematic issues. Later he became more proactive. He anticipated issues and looked for them. He identified four issues. One was the existence of competition by parents for various teachers. Another was the difficulty of establishing continuity in the curriculum. A third issue was difficulty in building teacher teams. The fourth problematic issue area was a lack of cooperation by one combination class teacher whenever the idea or concept at hand was not hers. As to the origin of the problematic issues, the principal paid only little attention to them. He believed that not much could be done about the origin and, therefore, seeing himself as a pragmatic person, he did not dwell on causes.

Using the same methods of looking at participants in the issues as he did when he looked at the issues themselves, Mr. Jackson detected the following participants: himself, the two combination grade teachers, some parents, some students who were aware of the jokes being told in one of the classes, and other teachers whenever a schoolwide issue was of concern. The principal found only himself and one of the teachers responsible for the issues: one of the teachers for causing them and himself for needing to tackle them.

The principal used two criteria to look at possible specific problems. One criterion was the situation when the problem involved children, such as the curriculum continuity problem. The second criterion was the situation when the problem involved a schoolwide effort, such as the "family" project. This project's goal was to promote empathy by sixth graders for the younger children. Mr. Jackson saw the first problem as owned by him and the reading teachers and the second one as owned by him only. He saw both problems as top priority for the school. There seemed to be two possible negative effects if the problems continued to exist: divisiveness of the teaching staff and a loss in his own credibility with teachers. The principal based these conclusions on his own experience, as well as on what teachers told him—that he must not allow such a lack of cooperation by one teacher. When questioned, he made no prediction about how the problems could be managed if they continued unresolved.

Finally, the principal decided to work on one problem. It was the new spelling curriculum in the combination class where the teacher had refused to use it. In search of alternative solutions, he structured a situation that called for a grade-level staff meeting. Teachers in grades one and two who had worked with the recalcitrant teacher were asked to apply peer pressure, with the aim of achieving a group consensus in the meeting. If unsuccessful, Mr. Jackson felt that he would have to talk directly to the teacher about it. He had identified these two possible alternative strategies from conversation with teachers, naming three direct owners of the solutions: himself, the reading teacher, and the other combination class teacher. It was a high priority for the principal to arrive at an effective solution. For the reading teacher and the other combination class teacher, it was important, but they could rationalize that it was the principal's decision.

Mr. Jackson also looked at the possible effects, cost, and manageability of the solutions. On the basis of his own assessment as to what would be a good solution and best consensus, he decided that to confront the teacher, both while informing her of what he wanted and afterward, would be appropriate. He felt that this was necessary for the sake of the children and that the teacher would go along. Historically, such approaches had worked for him in the absence of other viable alternatives. This teacher did not attend the meeting that he scheduled with all the grade-level teachers. So only one alternative was left—the direct one.

In conclusion, the principal decided on the solution of informing the teacher of what he wanted. He implemented his solution and the implementation process went well. The teacher was a conscientious person, and once she received personal attention, she reacted positively. It appeared that her need for praise was going to determine how she implemented the imposed solution. The principal's solution-implementation design involved asking other grade-level teachers to provide him with input about her work. He implemented this design and found the cost of implementing this design not to be high. It was hoped that this teacher would become part of the group—a team player —and that if she found out that they reported positively about her, she would then integrate herself more readily into the group.

CASE #12

*When the Number of Students to Be Enrolled
in the School Is Uncertain*

The principal, Mrs. Nora Dunn, has been in this school for
the past 2 years. Altogether, she has been a principal for 6 years.
The school enrolls 560 students. The problematic situation that
the principal mentioned first appeared in June, when teachers
received their teaching assignment for the following year. The
teachers and the principal knew that the assignments might
change as a function of the number of students. All agreed that
the chances were high that the number of students would decrease in kindergarten and increase in grades four and five. There
were legal limits to class size. Also, the district had severe budgetary problems. As to teachers, no one from the kindergarten
classes wanted to take an upper grade, and in the upper grade,
teachers and parents opposed combination classes. Fundamentally, the case involved personnel and student personnel issues
as well as budgetary issues.

Mrs. Dunn decided to observe and participate in the problematic situation. She uncovered problematic issues in discussions with some teachers and with the assistant superintendent. There could be 32 students in each of three kindergarten
classes. In the year before, there were less students in each of
four classes. It was possible that a kindergarten teacher would
have to be moved to either grade four or five. If there were
going to be four kindergarten classes, then combination grades
would have to be created all the way up as follows: first-second,
second-third, third-fourth, fourth-fifth, and fifth-sixth. The principal contemplated the origin of these issues. She suspected that
parents simply did not want combinations and that teachers
kept their solidarity intact as much as they could. Ultimately
she discussed the matter with all the teachers in the school
and also with the assistant superintendent and superintendent.
Mrs. Dunn viewed all of them as participants in the issues. She
also viewed herself and the teachers in kindergarten, fourth,
and fifth grades as responsible for the issues.

As the principal was sorting out potential specific problems to work on, she tentatively thought of how ineffective the weak kindergarten teacher would be in the upper grades. She also thought about how large the classes in the fourth and fifth grade should be. Although she talked extensively with the assistant superintendent about this, she saw only herself as the owner of these potential problems. These problems were placed at the top of her priority list because these problems involved many people. She viewed the effects of the problems as unsettling for teachers and was herself unsettled also. The school was only six students short of being able to hire another teacher but had to wait a week to find out if this were possible. The principal talked to the superintendent and learned that he would prefer giving her another teacher to seeing five combination classes created. She had two difficult weeks but she managed.

What problems did Mrs. Dunn choose to work on? One was the matter of increased enrollment. She decided to wait and gamble that six more students would enroll. The other approach was to try to convince the superintendent to give her another teacher in lieu of setting up five combination classes. She lobbied extensively with the assistant superintendent and the superintendent. For the superintendent, these problems were not at the top of his priority list. Money was his major consideration. For the assistant superintendent, one problem was paramount: that the weak kindergarten teacher not teach in the upper grades. For the principal, to get another teacher was of the highest priority. She refused to reassign the kindergarten teacher to the upper grades because the cost would be too high. She managed the uncertainty with difficulty but pretty well.

Mrs. Dunn's chosen solution was creating three combination classes as follows: third-fourth, fourth-fifth, and fifth-sixth. Although she talked three times with the superintendent, she received no additional teaching position. Therefore, she met with all the teachers and informed them that a decision had to be made in the school. Many of the teachers did not want to be involved in the decision, but the principal and the teachers felt that the solution she chose was the least of two evils. Although the principal felt that she managed the solution implementation process well, the cost of it was high. Some of the staff felt that it was unfair to create so many combination classes. Some community members also felt that it was wrong to create so many combination classes, so the principal met with these parents individually and in a group. She saw herself as the sole owner of this solution.

The principal decided to install a monitoring solution implementation design. For two to three weeks she checked with parents several times. She kept in contact with students and also asked the school psychologist to touch base with the students. Based on her talks with teachers and parents, she determined that this process has taken and will take time. Teachers' dislike of combination classes would be another cost. Two of the three combination classes were working well, but the third was not.

CASE #13

When the Teaching Staff Disagrees
About Bilingual Education's Value

Mr. Kenneth Rivera, the principal in this case, has been administering schools for 7 years, 2 in his present position. The school enrolls 740 students on two campuses. The problematic situation the principal recalled involved curriculum and personnel issues. There was dissatisfaction with the social and academic progress made by the Spanish-speaking students enrolled in the school's bilingual programs. The principal had tried to provide these students with social and academic offerings, but without much success. In addition, he even experienced resistance from some teachers and some parents as to the existence of bilingual classes. Objections were based on arguments associated with isolation of students. The principal, however, had to continue to provide the bilingual program for the Spanish-speaking students and was strongly committed to meeting their social and academic needs as well.

Mr. Rivera decided to observe and participate in the problematic situation, realizing that it was he who was creating the issues. After meeting with the bilingual and other teachers, he realized that the teaching staff was polarized. He also found out, after talking to parents, that the community was negative toward the program, and that attracting English-only students to the bilingual classes might be one direct solution that was impossible to achieve. In addition, the principal realized, after speaking briefly with district personnel, that the origin of the issues included mixed signals from the district about isolating many of the district's Spanish-speaking students in his school. The district seemed committed to providing bilingual programs but placed these classes in only two schools—his two-campus school and one other school. He viewed himself and his teaching staff as participants in the issue and only himself as responsible for the issue.

The principal was able to identify on his own possible specific problems he might work on. One was to develop a program of integration of the two groups of students. Another was to find and use symbolic time together. A third was to initiate a systematic evaluation of the needs and possible ways of meeting them. He saw himself as the sole owner of these possible problems and he considered them top priority. His concern focused on the negative effects of division among teachers and the possible relationship between unhappy teachers and the community. The major difficulty in managing these possible problems was not receiving full and exact information from teachers.

Mr. Rivera identified a problem to work on. It was the development of a program marked by integration between the two groups of students. Based on his meetings with teachers, he conceptualized a few possible solutions to the problem. One was a schoolwide exchange of programs in which students studied for 1 ½ hours every Thursday in a different instructional setting. Another was an exchange of students whereby English was taught to Spanish-speaking students for ½ hour every day. A third possible solution was that Spanish was taught to English-speaking students for ½ hour every day. The principal viewed himself and the first-, second-, third-, and fourth-grade teachers as owners of the possible solutions. He considered these possible solutions as part of his top three priorities in the school, and if the programs were implemented, he believed that their effect would be strong on the community. There would be much publicity about the integration. The only cost would be time and the only difficulty in managing the solutions would be managing student discipline due to a high rate of student turnover.

The principal decided to implement the three solutions mentioned above. He looked at the implementation process together with the teachers. He worked specifically with the bilingual teachers and presented the program to other teachers including its potential benefits. Some of the teachers saw the program as helpful and some as a barrier. Managing it became easier with time and the cost was not extensive. Mr. Rivera and the bilingual teachers owned the solution implementation process.

He also decided on a monitoring solution implementation design. A checklist was devised of evaluation questions and teachers were asked to answer them. In addition, he met every Thursday with grade-level teachers, separately with first and second, third and fourth, and fifth and sixth. The implementation of this design was costly in terms of time. Its effect led to strengthening the solutions themselves but also to splitting the teaching staff and to the increased use of indirect communication.

CASE #14

When Students' Homes Are Blamed for Student Failure in School

This principal, Mr. James Ferguson, has administered the current school for 3 years. The school enrolls 640 students. The principal reported on a problematic situation involving his teaching staff's negative attitudes when working with a multiethnic, low socioeconomic student population. The fundamental issues were associated with instruction, student personnel, and school-community relations. The principal decided to observe and participate in the problematic situation.

Mr. Ferguson first looked at the problematic issues and their origin. The teaching staff had a pattern of blaming the student home and family for problems at school. Some parents also exhibited a racist attitude. Both factors led to a situation in which it was difficult to attempt to change the teachers' negative attitudes without alienating them. After receiving much input from staff and parents, the principal became acquainted with all the participants in the issue. During meetings, he began to count the number of times that staff members mentioned the fault of the student homes. He also kept track of the number of times teachers referred students to the principal's office. The principal viewed himself as the only one responsible for the issues, even though at times he had no control over them.

Possible specific problems to work on were chosen as a result of extensive consultation with his advisory committee and the site council. Mr. Ferguson's essential problem was how to maximize student achievement, learning climate, student self-esteem, and a multicultural perspective on the part of all teachers at the school. He considered himself, the parents, and the students to be the owners of this problem. The teachers were not included because of their burnout and exhaustion. To work on the key problem was not of high priority for all owners, but for the principal it was of great import. He viewed the effects of the problem, if it were to linger, as bad: a continued split in the society between the haves and have-nots. The principal gave much consideration about whether or not to tackle this problem because he saw the manageability to be difficult.

Finally, Mr. Ferguson decided to work on achieving the goal. He chose to focus on creating a positive attitude on the part of all teachers toward all students in the school. The possible solution he chose after consulting with many individuals and groups of teachers and lay people was to model this positive attitude himself. He also chose to create a staff development plan. The owners of the plan were to include himself, teachers, his advisory committee, his school site council, and his student council. This priority was not high for all of the participants, but Mr. Ferguson worked on raising its prominence. He saw the solution of this problem as possibly creating a more positive environment. The cost included participant time and the salary of an outside consultant. The principal still saw the manageability as difficult.

Mr. Ferguson decided to begin with a staff development plan. After receiving input from several individuals and groups,

he began to discuss the plan at grade-level meetings, staff
meetings, and in student and lay group meetings. On his own,
he could not determine the effectiveness of the solution implementation process or its manageability. He expected the cost to
be high. He predicted that there would be many solution owners, including himself, teachers, parents, and students. Because
of the circumstances, he was not yet ready for solution implementation monitoring, even though he already knew how difficult it would be to measure change in attitudes.

CASE #15

When the Principal Believes
That the School's Image Requires Changing

The principal, Mr. Al Connell, has been administering schools
for 22 years. Two years ago the district superintendent asked
him to take over a school whose image had been suffering due
to perceived elements of racism, low student achievement scores,
and poor teaching. Of the school's current 590 students, 250 are
of Hispanic origin and 250 are English-only. Mr. Connell agreed
to take over the school on the condition that he would be given
a free hand. He believed that the school needed total overhaul,
not necessarily in replacing people but in changing the image.
He knew he would have to face a variety of issues, including
governance, curriculum, instruction, personnel, student personnel, budget, and school-community relations.

At the outset, the principal decided to observe and participate in the problematic situation in depth. He listened quite a
bit to hearsay. He heard that most teachers were alleged to be
less than enthusiastic about their jobs. There was a documented
white flight. Frequent comments were heard from individuals
in the community about the school's negative image. On the
basis of these observations and inputs, the principal determined
the problematic issues to be as follows: poor school image; a
racist attitude among the staff and in the community; lack of
understanding of the meaning of actual student achievement
scores; teaching staff that was not poor but had an image of being

poor; and a lack of information about the school in the school's community. The principal had learned about the origin of these issues from the way community members talked about the teaching staff and from the previous principal. He determined the origin of the issues to be lack of planning and lack of discipline. He also discovered a compounding variable: the closure of a nearby school.

Mr. Connell considered himself, his entire teaching staff, and the school's community to be participants in and responsible for the issues. He made this determination after having met with community leaders and teachers. He expected all those involved to take part in determining all of the major desired changes before working on any one of them.

On his own, the principal decided to work on the following problems: how teachers were seen; how to increase the visibility of outstanding teachers; how to help the few weak teachers to improve; how to inform the community about the school; and how to inform the real estate agents working in the school's attendance area about the school. He believed that the problems would be owned by himself and that the problems would be of top priority for him and for the teachers. Mr. Connell made the prediction that if the problems lingered, he would be personally disappointed, the teaching staff would become angry with him, and at least one teacher would bad-mouth him behind his back. He also predicted that he would be able to manage the problems well, especially if he began to study Spanish.

Mr. Connell decided to work on all five problems mentioned above. He assigned the highest solution priority to working with teachers on their image, visibility, and effectiveness. He also considered the neutralization of bad-mouthing of the school by people in the community to be very important. Possible programs were planned: using fraternity and sorority students from a nearby university as tutors of his students and inviting 45 to 50 real estate agents to learn about the school. Several other ideas he thought of on his own. Some came to him after meeting with teachers and community leaders. The principal believed that each person was the owner of a solution in which he or she participated. He viewed his role as that of a conductor of a symphony. He pushed hard for possible solutions, feeling that the solutions should be of the highest priority for himself, teachers, school site councils, school PTA, and others among parents and in the community.

Based on input from the community, individual parents, and his own examination, Mr. Connell thought that the possible effects of the proposed solutions would include raising the self-worth of bilingual teachers, making it impossible for parents to talk down bilingual education to the principal, and bringing to an end the divisiveness among the teaching staff. He believed that the cost of these solutions would include some time, some commitment, and three to four released days for all staff. Manageability was predicted to be quite possible.

The principal decided on all five solutions mentioned above and on their implementation. Based on discussions with teachers and on letters he received from people in the community, it seemed to him that the solution implementation process was proceeding but in an unpredictable manner. There was "go" and "stop." In the stop phase there was quite a bit of assessment. Some solutions were put on the back burner for a while, such as continued discussions with real estate agents. Based on the principal's own assessment, the solution process implementation proceeded fast and in a shocking way. The principal's high energy level explained, in part, the commitment he showed. He managed the process well, but he paid a high emotional cost. He believed that all concerned, and not he alone, owned the solution implementation process.

Mr. Connell decided on a monitoring solution implementation design and implemented it. Two teachers were selected by their colleagues to provide their input to the principal and the principal's input to them. Also, the principal communicated directly about progress to the school site council. The cost of the design implementation involved some time. From time to time the principal also discussed the progress with the district's director of bilingual education, who regularly informed the assistant superintendent and the superintendent. Goals had been accomplished, in part, after two years. Two new issues had unfolded. One was the desire to expand second language instruction in the school, meaning that a curriculum had to be prepared. The other was the desire to improve student test scores.

CASE #16

When Parents Resent Reputedly Weak Teachers

Mr. Michael Kirby, the principal in this case, began administering schools 11 years ago. His last 6 have been in this school, which enrolls 440 students. Before the end of the school year, this principal started to sense parental pressure for placement of children with various teachers in various grade levels. Pressure arose when it became clear that not all children could be placed as wished. Had he done exactly what the parents wanted, the principal would have created significant imbalance in the size and makeup of the classes as well as in the teaching loads. Teachers also felt pressure when parents simply contacted them directly. They preferred that the principal alone talk to parents about this issue. Teachers did not like to feel in competition with each other and they pressured the principal to do something about it. Mr. Kirby sensed that he had to do something, indeed. He faced personnel and student personnel issues as well as issues related to school-community relations.

Mr. Kirby decided to observe and participate in this problematic situation. As it turned out, he heard complaints about actual student placements as well as about the student placement process. Following dialogues with teachers and personal contemplation, the principal identified three problematic issues: One was the basis for student placement decisions. Another problem concerned the vehicle for parental input about their placement wishes. The third issue involved the procedure for communicating to the parents what the student placement decisions were. The principal explored the origin of these issues. His thoughts led him to the need to help weak teachers so that parents would not need to worry about them in the first place. He decided that he, the parents, and the teachers were participants in the issues and that he and the parents were responsible for the issues.

After considering possible specific problems, Mr. Kirby concluded the following: There was a need to clarify the ideology, method, and procedures of student placement. There was also a need to deal with the fallout from above. There was also a need to work on the language used in communicating information to parents. He knew that he was the sole owner of these problems but he thought that the teachers should also own them. In the spring, he placed these three needs on the top of his list of priorities as well as on the top of the teachers' list. He examined the possible effects of the problems and saw tension between himself and parents on one hand and between the teaching staff and himself on the other. As to manageability of the placement problems, he was hoping that the policy would continue to be useful. He knew, however, that the current policy had problems.

The principal chose a problem on which to work. It was the document that the school would publish regarding student placement policies. His goal was to clarify these policies. He saw the solution of the problem as being the policy clarification itself. At a teachers' meeting that he called to discuss the subject, some teachers advocated that parental complaints should be ignored. Other teachers and the principal believed that parental complaints needed to be attended to. The principal saw it as fulfilling the school's obligations to parents and to the public. None of the teachers offered to own the problem. The principal did, and he literally forced teachers to work on the document without owning it. To arrive at a satisfactory solution was his top priority. Looking at possible effects of the possible solutions, the principal considered the clarification of policy as enhancing his and the school's credibility. He consulted with the school site council and concluded that both continued parental pressure and an unclear policy would lead to loss of credibility. His examination of the cost of the solution led him to see that much time would have to be spent on this project, and much emotional stress would be experienced.

Mr. Kirby decided on a solution: namely, a one-page brochure that clarified student placement policy. He led the implementation process himself. There were three drafts. Teachers helped to go over the drafts and provided input. Finally, the principal mailed copies of the policy to the parents along with a letter stating that the policy on placement procedures was not new. He saw the communication as a clarification and its value as good management and good public relations. Feedback from parents on the product was good. Feedback from teachers on the process was also good. The solution implementation provided the principal with a strong basis on which to stand. He took questions and responded well. He used criteria from the brochure and defended them. It took time and energy, but he thought that time was well spent. Even though the teachers were involved in the solution implementation, the principal remained the sole owner of the solution and of the student placement policy itself.

In time, Mr. Kirby decided on a monitoring solution implementation design. In June he asked teachers about the existence of possible problems. He wanted to know the number of unhappy parents who felt that the procedure was not working and who were unhappy with the placement of their child. The cost of implementing this design was low. There was no need for staff meetings. The effectiveness of implementing the design was high. Even the school site council was interested in the number of incidences of parental unhappiness.

CASE #17

When a Teaching Aide Is Totally Ineffective

This principal, Mrs. Linda Lopez, has been administering the current school for 6 years. The school enrolls 440 students. The problematic situation that the principal recalled involved a personnel case—an instructional assistant who could not perform classroom duties adequately. The teacher in this classroom felt ineffective in dealing with the situation. This assistant had been problematic for several years. The principal decided to observe and participate in the problematic situation.

The principal first looked at problematic issues. Following discussions with people and her own classroom observations, the principal discovered that classroom control was lacking, increased demands on the teacher were causing negative effects on students, relationships between the teacher and the assistant were strained, and the principal herself was accused of racial discrimination. Documents showed that the assistant had health problems related to age and weight and that these problems caused the assistant to miss work repeatedly. Based on discussions with individuals and in groups, the principal determined that the assistant, the teacher, the students, herself, and the union were participants in the issues, and that all of the above (except students) were responsible for the issues.

Mrs. Lopez determined the existence of four specific problems: There was no classroom control; there was a lack of familiarity with the state framework; there were conflicts between the teacher and the assistant; and the assistant's attitude was poor. The principal felt that the assistant, the teacher, and principal herself owned these problems. Of high priority for the assistant was getting an answer to her question as to why she was being evaluated negatively at that time. Of high priority for the teacher was to manage the classroom and to help the assistant. High priority issues for the principal were identical to those of the teacher. If the problems lingered, the principal felt that the teacher's frustration would increase, the assistant's poor skills would be reinforced, and the negative effects on the students would intensify. She predicted difficult manageability of the problems if they lingered on and decided to focus work on the problem of classroom management.

Following discussions with all participants as well as the superintendent and the union representative, the principal thought of four possible solutions: Have the assistant observe other classes and do relevant readings; have the teacher work with her directly; change her job; and document inadequacies in order to start a termination process. The principal considered the assistant, the teacher, potential new teachers, the union, and herself as owners of the possible solutions. She knew that the assistant's top priority was to be with the children. She also knew that the teacher's priority was to give more specific directions, reduce the size of the groups, and remove the aide from the class. The priority of the principal was to facilitate improvement. The union wanted to avoid unfair practice.

Mrs. Lopez determined on her own that the possible effects of the solutions included the assistant moving to another job where the match would be better or supervisory interventions whereby the situation could be turned around. The principal also thought that a threat of termination might help the assistant's motivation. The cost of the solutions, according to the principal, was time to all participants and increase of teacher frustration if there was no change. Finding a new job for the assistant might also cause problems. The principal felt that all solutions were manageable, except, perhaps, for seeking termination.

The principal decided to move the assistant temporarily to a new assignment. She found teachers willing to work with her. Mrs. Lopez met with the assistant and the teachers separately and together. They discussed job expectations. The assistant was moved to the new position. The principal determined on her own that the solution was meant to be temporary. Therefore, the effectiveness of the solution implementation process would be high if a context could be created in which the assistant were successful and if the transition could be made smoothly. Based on discussions with all involved, Mrs. Lopez determined that manageability was satisfactory. The cost still involved quite a bit of time for everyone. The owners of the solution implementation process were the new teachers, principal, and the instructional assistant. The principal decided to monitor the solution implementation. The monitoring design included follow-up observations, increased documentation by teachers and the principal, and discussion with teachers regarding appropriate evaluations of assistants. The principal implemented the design. The cost of monitoring involved teachers' and principal's time. The effectiveness of the monitoring would be good if it could show improvement or termination.

CASE #18

When a Disabled Teacher Can No Longer Teach Effectively

This new principal, Mrs. Mary Wilcox, has just completed her first year on the job. Her school enrolls 410 students. As soon as she started working, she realized that one of her two special education teachers was in an advanced stage of physical and mental disability. The teacher had already lost her ability to read aloud and had experienced a significant loss of memory. Student behavioral problems had increased in her class and parents had expressed an increased concern. The other special education teacher had pointed to several inadequate instructional situations. Some of the staff in the school had become angry with the disabled teacher over scheduling problems such as not being on time. Various problematic incidences related to her classroom. However, other staff members in the school were forgiving of her inadequacies and had developed a strong sense of loyalty to her. The case involved instructional, personnel, and budgetary issues.

Mrs. Wilcox decided to observe and participate in the problematic situation. She had already known the teacher before, as they had once taught together in another school. The teacher's previous principal had written a report about her and the current principal consulted this report heavily. She exchanged a lot of information with the district's director of special education about the teacher. She also held many discussions with the teacher. Several issues and problems were identified. From records it was clear that the teacher had once been quite strong and that she had been sent to this school from her previous school only this year. The principal in the former school had dealt with the teacher as if not much was wrong with her.

The principal of this current school viewed herself, the district's special education director, the disabled teacher, and the teacher's classroom aide as participants in the issues. She viewed only herself and the special education director as being responsible for the issues. In extensive discussions with the teacher, the principal monitored her planning activities as well as her communication with parents. This monitoring convinced the principal that the owners of the problem included herself, the district's director of special education, and the district's director of personnel. For all three, the problem was very high on their priority list. Mrs. Wilcox discussed the situation with the two district directors extensively. She saw potential negative effects of the problem, including a significant number of this teacher's 11 students being removed from this school by their parents. She also saw an increase in physical disability including an inability to handle physical objects; once the teacher even fell out of her wheelchair.

The principal decided to work on two specific problems. One was to monitor the teacher's instructional activity and communication with the parents. The other was to monitor her physical condition. Mrs. Wilcox now consulted regularly with the teacher, her aide, and the district's director of special education. She looked at alternative solutions and prepared checklists to use on a regular basis. She also transferred some activities from the teacher to her aide. In addition, she sent notes to the special education director, the teacher, and the aide on a regular basis, summarizing what information was being looked at. All four of them became potential owners of the solutions. All but the teacher saw the solutions as important. The teacher did not. Her husband applied pressure on everyone for her to be able to continue as long as possible, but data showed that she was losing her memory and information-processing ability. Relations between the principal and the teacher remained good. The cost of the monitoring activities was high in terms of time, but manageability of the interim solutions was satisfactory, although difficult.

Mrs. Wilcox decided to work with the teacher for a little while longer and then to tell her that she could no longer continue to work. She discussed it with the district director of special education and with the aide. All three agreed that the solution implementation process was not very effective. They felt that the teacher was being allowed to continue longer than was advisable, that the principal had allowed too much inadequate teaching to go on. The manageability of the implementation was difficult. The cost was high. The owners of the process at this point remained the principal and the director of special education. This was in February. The teacher left at that point and did not return to the classroom until May (to return the key), when the "administrative leave" became "retirement." The continued dialogue between the two women produced some monitoring solution implementation that was low in cost and high in effectiveness. Finally, the teacher accepted her fate and the principal looked for another special education teacher.

CASE #19

When Students Want to Demonstrate Outside of the Campus

The principal, Dr. Todd Driscoll, has administered this middle school for the past 2 years. The school enrolls 653 students in grades seven and eight. There is one vice-principal at the school.

The principal faced a problematic situation that involved issues of curriculum, student personnel, and school-community relations. Students had to be kept from marching off campus as a sign of a protest in reaction to the first Rodney King verdict. The principal decided to observe and participate in the problematic situation. He considered the problematic issues to be a desire by students to be highly visible. He also saw the need to have the school's main exits patrolled. The source of the students' desire to demonstrate was one student leader and a small group of vocal followers who convinced a large number of students to march.

After consulting with the vice-principal, the principal considered the following participants to be involved in the issues: the student leader, the teaching staff, the neighborhood, and the local business community. Those responsible were the student leader and the students who wished to participate. The possible problems to work on were the control of students and the need to patrol the main gates. All of the named participants were considered owners of the problems. Each one's priority—to march or to avert student participation in the march—was high. The principal saw the effect of the problem if it were allowed to linger as the disruption of local business. The manageability of the problem was difficult due to the small teacher-student ratio.

Dr. Driscoll decided to work on two specific problems. One was to keep students on campus and the other was to redirect their anger into an alternative, more positive, format. He consulted with the vice-principal, the student adviser, and students and discussed with them the possible solutions of blocking the school exits and coming up with alternative sets of activities for the students. He viewed the teaching staff and student body officers as owners of the possible solutions and he saw their top priority as keeping students in classes. He believed that holding discussions in classes would calm students down, and that they would then not be as interested in marching off campus. The cost of implementing this possible solution was going to involve the equivalence of 2 days of substitute teachers.

Because the manageability of this possible solution was considered difficult due to lack of additional needed personnel, the principal (in consultation with the vice-principal) felt that another, more dramatic and visible event had to take place. Accordingly, the principal decided to encourage the students to hold a rally in the auditorium and to invite guest speakers.

The rally took place. It had a moderate effect, but the auditorium was full. Some students found it an opportunity to cut class. The manageability of the solution implementation process was satisfactory. The principal considered the cost to be moderate—supervision time, primarily. He considered himself, the vice-principal, the student adviser, the student leader, and the student body officers as owners of the solution implementation process. Dr. Driscoll's choice of a solution monitoring design was attendance in the rally. The cost of implementing this design was minimal. Its effectiveness was high. It involved large numbers of students, a way for students to express themselves, and the avoidance of a march off campus.

CASE #20

When Misbehavior of Students Becomes Excessive

In this case involving personnel and student personnel issues, the principal, Mr. Warren Strickland, has administered the school for 3 years. The school enrolls 600 students. There is also an assistant principal at the school. The principal considered a problematic situation in which the teaching staff complained of massive student misbehavior and parents expressed concerns about the safety of their children and their lack of academic achievement. The principal decided to observe and participate in the problematic situation.

After observing and listening for a while, the principal sorted out the problematic issues. He noted that there had been high numbers of suspensions for unacceptable behavior, incidences of lack of respect for the school building and grounds (including vandalism after school hours), lack of motivation to achieve academically, excessive tardiness, and excessive absenteeism. He also detected resulting teachers' morale problems. His conclusions about the origins of the problematic situation were changes in the demography and the style of the previous principal.

After discussing participation and responsibility with a variety of individuals and groups, the principal saw a large number of individuals as participants in the issues and as being responsible for them, including the assistant principal, the teachers, the students, the parents, community people, and the police. He selected the following possible specific problems to work on: attendance, tardiness, vandalism, achievement, and attitudes. Mr. Strickland considered the students to be the owners of these problems, yet he had problems himself in determining how high in the students' priorities was the need to attend to these problems. The principal was, nonetheless, confident that the problems needed to be attended to because otherwise things would get worse and unmanageable.

Mr. Strickland chose to work on all areas of concern: disciplinary issues, tardiness, absenteeism, vandalism, lack of respect, and low achievement. He examined a particular STAR program that was being administered in a city 3 hours away, and, with a group of five teachers, he traveled to see STAR in operation. The principal realized that the owners of STAR were teachers, aides, counselors, administrative staff, and support staff. The high priority of all concerned was to attend to and solve the problems. Back at his school, Mr. Strickland held group discussions. Almost everyone in the school thought that if STAR were implemented at their school, improvement was possible. The principal himself was certain that improvement would occur. As to costs, he saw a need for only $4,000 for staff time in the first year and $2,000 in the second year. He predicted no problems in the manageability of this possible solution.

STAR was implemented throughout the school. The five original teachers who had observed in the other school worked with the rest of the staff (with the help of the principal) on solution implementation. Attendance and tardiness improved in one year. Vandalism stopped almost completely. A positive atmosphere was developing in the school. Manageability of the solution implementation required only 15 minutes at the beginning of each school day. The actual cost turned out to be exactly what had been predicted. Students, as well as parents and the community, became the solution implementation process owners. The monitoring solution implementation design included review of attendance and punctuality records, record of vandalism, and end-of-the-year survey about attitudes. It did not include student achievement. The cost of the monitoring solution implementation also involved only 15 minutes per day on the part of each teacher. The monitoring effectiveness was high.

CASE #21

When the Behavior of a Student Becomes Unacceptable

Mr. Jean McElroy, the principal in this student personnel case, has administered the school for 25 years. The school enrolls 605 students. It has one assistant principal. The problematic situation involved an eighth grader who had been disruptive and who lacked discipline, motivation, parental support, and respect for himself, other people, and the school rules. The principal decided to observe and participate in this problematic situation. He had past experience with the eighth grader's family and had discussed it with teachers, both formally and informally. Mr. McElroy determined that there were several problematic issues with the student, as follows: He had disrupted classes and activities; he had hampered the learning of other students; he did not complete his own work; teachers did not want him in their classes; he was disliked by other students; and his parents had been difficult to deal with. The origin of the issues appeared to include the alcoholism of his parents and their lack of self-respect and discipline. The principal saw the students, teachers, and others who had been in contact with the eighth grader, as well as himself, as participants in the issues. He saw himself as the responsible party in this case.

Relying on his experience and discussions with teachers, the principal determined some possible problems to work on, including improving the student's social skills and having him learn the importance of rules, responsibility, and something about the society. Mr. McElroy felt that he owned these problems and that getting the student to stop the disruptive behavior was his top priority in this case. He saw nothing but serious additional problems emerging if these problems lingered on. He could not predict how manageable the problems would be.

The principal decided to keep the student from disrupting classes and activities at school. After much consultation, he examined first the school behavior policy that was already in place, whereby (a) students and parents make a contract to meet expectations; (b) students are isolated from peers at lunchtime; (c) students are removed from classes; and (d) students are removed from school for a half day. Mr. McElroy felt that he alone was the owner of these possible solutions. Succeeding with this particular eighth grader was a high priority for him.

The principal examined and considered the effects of the solutions. He discovered that the disruptive student had flunked several units of study and lacked various opportunities to learn. Also, there seemed to be no opportunities for him to acquire social skills. The cost in terms of principal time was high, but the solutions appeared to be manageable.

Mr. McElroy decided to use the school behavior policy that was in place. He and the student negotiated the contract of expected behaviors. With the help of teachers and staff he sent and administered four warnings, a letter to the parents, six additional warnings, a conference with the student and his parents, eight more warnings, and a removal of the student from classes. The principal thought that the solution implementation process would take time but would be manageable and would work. He thought that until something significant was done (change in the student's behavior or removal of the student) the cost would be high in the classes the eighth grader attended. He felt that he would be the sole owner of the solution implementation process. As described above, the principal used the standard school behavior monitoring system. The cost was high. Effectiveness was high, too.

CASE #22

When the School Does Not Comply
With a Bilingual Master Plan

This case occurred in a large middle school with 1,340 students and two assistant principals. The principal, Ms. Cynthia Johnson, had administered schools for 7 years, but it was her first year in the current school. Several issues came into play: governance, curriculum, instruction, personnel, student personnel, budgeting, and school-community relations. The problematic situation involved citations that the school had received repeatedly in the last 2 years for noncompliance in several areas with the district's bilingual master plan. The citations were in the area of staffing, testing, and parental notification and consent. Also, the school did not employ a coordinator for bilingual education because funding was insufficient to support this position. The district now required full compliance within 90 days. The principal decided to observe and participate in this problematic situation.

The state review team and district advisers informed the principal about the key problematic issue, which was a shift in the Spanish-speaking population of the school in the last 5 years from 15% to 85%. The state evaluation team informed the principal that the related issue was an increase in limited-English-proficient (LEP) students. Periodic compliance reviews involved the following as participants in the issue: district personnel, site administrators, bilingual teachers, parents, and students. The state review team and district personnel informed the principal that district personnel were responsible for the issue. Based on extensive discussions between the principal and district personnel, it was suggested that the possible problems to work on would be aggressive recruiting of bilingual personnel and a corresponding review and restructuring of the budget. District personnel owned these problems. It was of the highest priority to attend to these two problems for both the principal and district personnel. If the problems lingered there would be loss of funding and budget deficits. All district advisers agreed that the manageability would be feasible.

The principal decided that the main problem to work on was the inadequate bilingual staffing. The principal discussed with district advisers and bilingual teachers how to recruit such staff. She also dismissed the possible assignment of bilingual coordination responsibilities to the existing Title I coordinator. The owners of these possible solutions were the principal and district personnel. In a general meeting of all concerned it was agreed that the top priority was to comply with the master plan. They saw the effects of these solutions as increasing the academic achievement of the LEP students. The cost was to be a $1,500 to $5,000 stipend for each bilingual person recruited. Manageability was going to involve personnel training and monitoring, which would add to the cost.

The principal decided to consolidate the bilingual coordinator's responsibilities with the Chapter I coordinator position, as well as to hire additional bilingual teachers. Ms. Johnson suggested these solutions to district personnel and to the area superintendent. With input from bilingual advisers, she concluded that the effectiveness of the solution would be high. With input from advisers and teachers she believed that the manageability would be feasible. The cost was estimated as it was estimated in the last paragraph. The owners of the solution implementation process were the principal and one of her district bilingual advisers.

Ms. Johnson decided to design and implement a monitoring system: the school's administrative team, which was to meet, collect data, and interact with district personnel. Based on extensive consultations she determined the cost of the monitoring system to include personnel time. She saw the effectiveness of the system as high because of the high stakes and the genuine efforts to meet the goals.

CASE #23

When Major Cuts Have to Be Made

This assistant principal, Mr. George LeDoux, was one of three in a school that enrolled 2,050 students in grades 9 through 12. This was his fourth year in administration and at the current school. The problematic situation involved a need to eliminate nine classes and two substitute teachers in the face of the numbers of students in social studies classes. This situation involved budgetary, personnel, and instructional issues. The assistant principal decided to observe and participate in the problematic situation.

After consulting with the principal, the counselors, the principal again, the head counselors, the cochairs of the social studies department, the social studies teachers, and the principal again, the assistant principal determined the problematic issues to be as follows: Two substitute teachers had to be terminated; student schedules were disrupted; the bilingual program was disrupted; and there were difficulties in getting reasonable ratios of students to teachers in social studies classes. The origin of these issues was overstaffing. Mr. LeDoux determined that the students, some teachers, counselors, the departments of social studies and bilingual education, and the school administrators were participants in and responsible for the issues. After consulting with the principal, he concluded that the specific problems to work on were attainment of reasonable student-teacher ratios, elimination of nine classes and two teachers, and selection of which classes and teachers to eliminate. He saw himself as the sole owner of these problems. He considered as his top priority the need to affect the least possible number of students and staff. If the problems lingered, he saw them continuing to waste instructional and administrative time. He saw the manageability of the problems as difficult because many people did not understand them.

Mr. LeDoux decided to correct the student-teacher ratio in social studies and bilingual classes. He consulted the same parties as before and decided to implement what he had planned before:

cut nine classes, let two teachers go, and correct the ratio. He saw himself as the owner of this possible solution and also as the one who needed to affect as few people as possible. He predicted complaints by some parents, students, and teachers about the loss of some academic time. He also predicted resistance by the two substitute teachers who were to lose their jobs. The assistant principal saw the cost of the potential solutions as involving primarily loss of student academic time, administrative time, and teacher time. After consultation with the principal, he predicted that the solution implementation would be manageable.

The operational decisions that took place were cutting nine classes and letting two substitute teachers go. Before the solution implementation began, the assistant principal consulted again with the same parties as before. He then chose two teachers to cut, arranged to have other teachers compensate for lost staff, adjusted some student schedules, and made sure that everyone knew why the changes had been made and how. The assistant principal believed that the solution implementation process was effective and manageable, even if it were to require quite a bit of cooperation from students and teachers. He saw two costs. One was time for implementation. Another included some shifting around in the bilingual department. He saw himself as owning the entire solution implementation process.

Mr. LeDoux decided to design and implement a monitoring solution implementation system. He computerized the data for checking the schedule changes and he also met with classes involved to make sure that everyone understood the changes. The cost of monitoring involved some of his time and some student academic time. The monitoring effectiveness was high, and he found that the transition was smooth.

CASE #24

When a Student Attendance Policy Is Problematic

The assistant principal, Mrs. Shari Groves, has been in her present job for 18 years. The school includes grades 9 through

12 and enrolls 950 students. It also employs another assistant principal. The problematic situation included personnel and student personnel issues. It involved a strict student attendance policy that resulted in grades being lowered after a prescribed number of absences. Students and parents could appeal to the assistant principal. Students were upset by the policy. Many parents objected to it. The assistant principal found herself spending an enormous amount of time on the appeal process. The students finally staged a walkout of classes and a demonstration rally in the commons area of the school. Mrs. Groves decided to observe and participate in the problematic situation.

As a result of listening to student, parent, and teacher feedback, the assistant principal sorted out the following two problematic issues: Students with legitimate absences were penalized and Spanish-speaking students were disenfranchised. She also was aware of the excessive time it took to carry out the appeal process. The origin of these issues was the lowering of grades of students due to absences, including excused ones. The assistant principal viewed the following people as participants in the issues and as responsible for them: students, parents, teachers, assistant principals, and the principal.

After consulting with individuals and groups in the school, Mrs. Groves decided that the problems to work on were changing the attendance policy and maintaining good attendance. She viewed the owners of these two problems to be the same individuals as before. The problem was top priority for students and for the assistant principal. For her such a change would also constitute a lowering of the workload. She believed that the problem should not linger on and that changing the policy was manageable, but maintaining good attendance was in doubt.

The assistant principal decided to work on changing the attendance policy while maintaining attendance. After discussing the problem with the faculty advisory committee, the school site council, students, and administrators, she came up with the following possible solutions: Parents would need to phone the school when a student was absent; attendance coordinator would make home calls (telephone or visit); there would be Saturday school for unexcused absences; and there would also be a new form for teachers to complete, delineating absences and tardiness. Mrs. Groves saw as owners of the possible solutions all those mentioned earlier as responsible for the issues, plus the attendance coordinator. For all concerned these were top priorities. Students would not have grades lowered. Teachers would share in the decision making. Parents would have direct contact with the school. The workload of the assistant principal would be lowered. In addition, she thought of the following possible effects: lowered attendance rates, a larger load for the attendance coordinator, and large attendance in Saturday school. The cost would involve expanded time for the coordinator and a new position of Saturday school supervisor. The assistant principal thought that the solutions would be manageable but would require much effort due to the connection of attendance to Saturday school classes.

At this point the assistant principal decided to change the attendance policy. She did so after discussing it individually with other administrators in the school. As the solution implementation process proceeded, she became concerned with negative effects such as lower attendance and problems with manageability such as slow communication between the attendance coordinator and Saturday school. Lower attendance would mean lower ADA funding. Communication problems would mean a breakdown in policy change implementation. She considered the owners of the solution implementation process to be the same people mentioned before.

Mrs. Groves decided to design and implement a system of monitoring the process of the solution implementation. She examined the absences at the end of the semester, student by student, and especially those with numerous absences who still received a passing grade. She also examined ADA in detail. Based on her experience and on discussions with the other administrators in the school, she determined that the only monitoring cost was her time. The effectiveness of the monitoring system would be in tracking students with absences who were still receiving passing grades. This, she felt, was very important to the school.

CASE #25

When a Severely Disabled Student Enrolls in the School

This is a case of an assistant principal, Ms. Jessica Swaminathan, who has administered the current school for 3 years. The school has 1,600 students and one other assistant principal. The problematic situation involved a severely disabled student who appeared at the school on the first day of the year without records or any other documents or written information. The student and her parents insisted that she begin studying with everyone else. The assistant principal, whose responsibilities included special education and management of the school, had to investigate what type of program the student should have and how the school could best meet the student's needs. The case involved many issues including curriculum, instruction, governance, personnel, student personnel, budget, and student-community relations.

Ms. Swaminathan decided to observe and participate in the problematic situation. Having been notified by the office staff and the counselor of the quadriplegic student (who used a motorized wheelchair), the assistant principal investigated and found out from the student and her parents that she had been confined to a wheelchair since birth and that she needed assistance with basic needs such as eating, toileting, and dressing. Next, Ms. Swaminathan discussed the problematic issues with the special education staff. She considered as participants in the issues this staff, the counselors, the student, and her parents. She also saw them as those responsible for the issues.

On the basis of these discussions with various individuals, Ms. Swaminathan determined that the immediate problems that needed attention were: in which classes to enroll the student, who would assist her with her basic needs, and how to reassign aides' duties so that the student would have help. The assistant principal discussed ownership of the problems with the site special education coordinator and the district special education director, as well as with the aides assigned to the student. The initial priorities of the aides were to help in feeding and toileting. But problems mounted. The staff demonstrated frustration with the problem. The aides approached their union about their duties. The assistant principal was in communication with the district special education director and reported to him that the situation was becoming unmanageable.

Ms. Swaminathan decided to focus initially on getting the student's records, talking to the student's previous school, and putting together an interim plan that would enroll the student in the right classes with the right kind of assistance. She convened a meeting with the student's previous teacher, site special education staff, and the student's parents to discuss the best interim plan. The group agreed on classes and on who should provide the physical support. One special education coordinator, one special education teacher, and two aides would have to be assigned the responsibility for this possible solution. It became clear, however, that the student's priority was to become mainstreamed. Multiple discussions occurred after the realization that priorities differed. The effects, therefore, were viewed as varied. There was some successful integration but not in all areas. The cost of the possible solution involved aide time. In the long term a staff person would have had to be hired to work with this student. Both the assistant principal and her special education staff questioned their ability to manage the needs of the student.

The assistant principal decided that the immediate solution was to enroll the student in some mainstream classes with special education support and also to enroll her in some special education classes. In addition, an aide was assigned to the student to assist her with eating and toileting. These decisions were made after a meeting with all the participants. The staff agreed, with reservations, about enrollment in various assigned classes, but the aide assigned to assist with eating and toileting resisted her duties and complained to the union. The effectiveness of the solution implementation process suffered. The student required extensive time from the staff. The aide became uncooperative. Manageability was difficult. The short-term cost increased in terms of people's time. The district special education director was notified of all of this. The owners of the solution implementation process remained the special education resource teacher and the aide.

The assistant principal decided on a solution monitoring system. She implemented a monitoring method whereby the special education coordinator submitted a weekly report to the assistant principal and the two of them would meet subsequently. Following discussions with the special education staff, the assistant principal determined that there was a cost in people's time associated with the monitoring system but that the effectiveness of the system was high.

CASE #26

When Classes Are Overcrowded

In this case the high school is small: 650 students. The assistant principal, Mr. Brian McNeil, has been in the present job for only a year. There is another assistant principal in this school. The problematic situation involved three classes that had enrollments over the number allowed by the teachers' union contract. There were issues of instruction, personnel, and student personnel. The school had 30 days to correct the situation. The assistant principal decided to observe and participate in the problematic situation.

Written class lists were brought by the teachers to the assistant principal, who then brought them to the attention of the principal. There were at least three issues: how to adjust class size, how to approach individual teachers, and how to interpret the vague wording of the union contract. The origin of the problematic situation occurred in the spring, when the assistant principal met with the budget committee to discuss deficit spending and recommend layoff of three teachers. Based on discussions with the principal and teachers, the assistant principal saw himself, the teachers, the students, and the union as participants in the issues. He saw the responsibility for the issues as shared by him, the union, and the district.

Possible specific problems to work on included the large class sizes, the conflict with the union, and the concern of the teachers. The owners of these problems were the same as those of the issues. Mr. McNeil saw that it was up to himself and the union to resolve the contract violation and that it was a high priority to do so. The teachers' priority was to reduce class size. The students' priority was effective education. The assistant principal believed that if the problems lingered, the union would file a grievance and the teachers would grow increasingly unhappy. He speculated that in order to manage the problems the union would have to be satisfied.

The assistant principal decided to work on the union conflict over class size. After rereading the written contract and consulting again with the principal and the union president, he considered five possible solutions: have teachers sign off on overenrollment, move students to other classes, wait teachers out and have them sign off at crunch time, wait and hope for natural student attrition, and avoid the situation and hope for smaller enrollment in the future. He decided that the owners of these possible solutions would be himself, teachers, students, and parents. His priorities were either to approve teachers' requests about moving students out or wait until teachers make requests. He did not prefer to initiate action. The teachers' priority was to have the marginal students move out. The union's priority was to reduce class size. The assistant principal believed that the possible effects of the solutions might be happier teachers, unhappy teachers if large class size were to be maintained, satisfied union, union grievance if teachers signed off, and parents and students unhappy with midyear moves. He predicted time cost for himself, the teachers, the parents, and the union. He also speculated student cost associated with disruption in learning and schedules. Due to his ability to work cooperatively with the teachers, he foresaw good manageability of the solution.

The solution chosen by the assistant principal was to wait until the end of the 30-day period and only then to implement the solutions he had planned. He expected that either the teachers would sign off or that he would move the students to other classes. Based on one discussion with the principal and another one with the involved teachers, he began the 30-day waiting period. He came to the teachers without a plan for moving students, hoping that they would sign off. He also looked at students' records, including success in school, classes needed, and type of support needed. Also considered were the best student-class fit for each student and the actual moving of the students. Mr. McNeil knew that parents would object to a move of their students to other classes. The assistant principal managed well, however. He risked anger from both sides. A move of the students would anger the parents. A teacher sign-off could probably produce a union grievance. He was hoping for a sign-off without a grievance. The cost of the solution implementation process involved time and anxiety. The owners of the process included himself, the teachers, the students, and the parents. In his case, the assistant principal saw no need for monitoring the solution implementation process.

CASE #27

When a School Community Faces Negative Publicity

The school in question contains grades 10, 11, and 12 and enrolls 1,950 students. The principal, Mrs. Pat Ibarra, has administered this school for 10 years. Currently she has four assistant principals. The problematic situation involved the effects of gunshots that had been fired off campus during a school football game but that the media reported as having been fired on campus. The school's image had become negative and the school community had difficulties in addressing the negative publicity about the school. Students had problems coping and responding to the media. Complex developments occurred. There were school-community issues. There were curriculum issues. There were personnel and student personnel issues.

The principal decided to observe and participate in the problematic situation. She considered on her own that the single most important problematic issue was the need to address the negative publicity in the school and in the surrounding community. Based on her discussions with the athletic director and football coaches she saw that the issue originated when another high school refused to play the school in its facility and preferred a neutral field. *Sports Illustrated* magazine and local newspapers connected the school's refusal to play in this high school's facility with the shooting incident. Because the coaching personnel as well as students and parents in this other school knew that the shooting had not taken place in the playing facility, yet they refused to play there, the principal considered the students, parents, coaches, athletic directors, and the two principals in both schools as participating in the issue. She also thought that all of these participants were responsible for the issue.

The major possible specific problems the principal wanted to work on were the restoration of parent and student confidence through a positive media campaign and the implementation of additional security. The owners of the first problem were going to be high school officials who would be designated. The owner of the second problem was going to be the principal herself. These were going to be her top priorities. The principal reasoned that if the problems remained unsolved, the school's reputation would suffer greatly. The sports program and other extramural programs would be hurt, too. She saw the manageability of these possible problems to be difficult because of the volatility of public opinion.

The principal decided to concentrate on students first. She preferred this approach as a result of having met with faculty and parents. There she was told students were being continuously contacted by the media about the situation. Her goal was to conduct student forums in which she would stress the importance of being careful about what was said to the media. Another possible solution she considered was investigating counterstrategies to use by students and parents, such as writing articles and sending them to newspapers and magazines. She met with the faculty and assigned the task of working with students writing to the journalism and English teachers. She also assigned the task of improving the public relation dimension to athletic department personnel. Mrs. Ibarra considered the teaching and coaching staffs as owners of the respective possible solutions. These tasks were to become top priorities. The principal saw these possible solutions as producing positive effects on students (self-esteem) and staff, as well as on the school as a whole. Staff and students' time and some office expenditures were to be included as costs. She saw the manageability of the possible solution as relatively simple.

The chosen decision involved a series of meetings with students, parents, teachers, and administrators to discuss and suggest the variety of possible solutions mentioned above. Providing additional security was going to be the most manageable solution, but costly. The media campaign had the potential to be effective but could possibly be slow in achieving positive effects. The principal kept in close contact with district officials about all pertinent activities but considered herself, the athletic director, students, teachers, and parents as owners of the solutions. When interviewed, the principal had not yet decided on a monitoring solution implementation design.

CASE #28

When School Leadership Has Been Lacking

This principal, Mr. Kim Sun, is new to the high school, which includes grades 9 through 12 and enrolls almost 2,000 students. Mr. Sun has two assistant principals. He has served as an administrator for a total of 15 years. Prior to his joining the current school, there had been no stable leadership for over a year. Old problems became worse and new problems appeared. Chronic tardiness intensified. Incidences of students skipping class increased. Physical violence erupted. Vandalism intensified. Charges of racism were made. Parental concern for student safety increased. Most of the respect for authority was gone. This problematic situation involved a lack of order and control in school. There were personnel and student personnel issues as well as issues associated with school-community relations. The principal decided to observe and participate in the problematic situation.

Several individuals and groups approached the new principal. Each person and group expressed their concerns to him. These included the superintendent, the teachers, parents, and various community groups. The principal studied the issues of student behavior and academic problems. He also investigated alleged teaching staff apathy. The origin of the issues seemed to be in a relaxation of discipline by the teachers in the previous year and in blatant expressions of racism. The principal determined that without strong leadership in the school, the participants in the issues included teachers, students, and older gang members. He felt that the school administrators were responsible for allowing the issues to reach the level they did.

Originally, the principal chose to focus on the possibility of enclosing the campus with a fence and on improving class attendance. After consulting with several groups and individuals he decided that he and the assistant principals were the owners of these possible problems. He asked several people about priorities and learned that safety was the top priority for everyone. If the problem lingered, the effects would be damaging. The principal was hopeful about the manageability of these problems, but he was also sure that it would take a long time to turn things around.

Ultimately, the principal decided to work on safety, class attendance, punctuality, and staff apathy. He asked various groups about possible solutions. The consensus was that the campus had to be more secure, that attendance and punctuality should be strictly enforced, and that noncompliance should be consequential. He delegated the work on security to the assistant principals. He delegated student issues to the teachers. He also thought of a Saturday work program. Thus, there were several possible solution owners with high priorities. Mr. Sun thought of positive effects of these possible solutions. The cost would include his time, the time of the assistant principal, security personnel salaries, and 4 hours of a teacher's salary for the Saturday program. The principal believed that the solutions would take time and that they were manageable.

He decided to erect a fence around the campus, leaving three points of entrance. He also initiated the use of required parking permits and ordered the student parking lots locked during the day, except for noon. In addition he began the practice of suspending students for attendance and punctuality problems, initiated the work program for serious offenders, and identified teachers who were not enforcing the system. Based on

consultations with individuals in the school, he began the solution implementation process.

Students resisted the closing of the campus. Not all of the
staff complied. He thought that the new policies were effective,
nonetheless. Solution manageability was difficult because of
this resistance and also due to misunderstandings in the community. Manageability improved after a month. The school site
council funded the Saturday work program. The district's central office funded the increase in security. Time was the other
cost: his time and the time of the assistant principals. Mr. Sun
considered the administrators and teachers as owners of the
solution process.

The principal and the staff decided to monitor the solution
implementation process. They reviewed attendance and punctuality records on a weekly basis. They also initiated discussions with the teaching staff every 2 weeks. Mr. Sun met also
with community groups to discuss solutions. Clerical and counseling staff helped in reviewing records. The principal spent
some time monitoring the halls. No other cost was involved in
the monitoring process, which turned out to be highly effective.

CASE #29

When Students Are Suspended and a Mother Complains

Mr. John Prince is a new principal of a 4-year high school,
which enrolls 1,250 students and has two assistant principals.
The problematic situation involved two female students, each
suspended for 3 days due to a fight they had in front of the office
of the assistant principal. One student's mother complained
that her daughter should not have been suspended. The assistant principal turned the case over to the principal. The principal saw here student personnel issues and issues associated
with school-community relations. The principal decided to observe and participate in the problematic situation.

Using his past experience as an assistant principal, the principal sorted out the situation to identify the following problematic issues: the violation of the no-foul-language policy, the

danger of the situation, the need for a safe environment, and the need to back up the authority of the assistant principal. Together with the assistant principal, the principal determined the origin of the issues to be the fight over a boyfriend and the mother's complaint about the suspension. He included as participants in the issues the two students, their parents, the assistant principal, and the school as a whole. Because everyone on campus knew of the incident the principal considered all adults on campus responsible for the issues.

As an example to others, Mr. Prince decided to consider two problems to work on: to improve the language used by the two students involved in the fight and to change the mother's attitude about the situation. He saw himself owning these possible problems. His priorities were to stick to the suspension and to help the mother accept it. He felt that if the problems lingered, their effects on the school would be negative. He thought that the problems would be manageable.

The two problems the principal chose to work on were the suspension imposed by the assistant principal and the need to calm the mother. He asked the assistant principal for the facts and considered reducing the suspension to one or two days or dropping the suspension altogether. Another possible solution was to induce the mother to accept the suspension. The principal considered himself as the owner of these possible solutions. His solution priorities were to let the students know that they did wrong and to back the authority of the assistant principal. These were high priorities for him. He determined that the effects of the possible solutions could include either the district office overruling the suspension and damaging his authority, or if the suspension were upheld, discouraging other students from fighting. The major cost he saw was going to involve authority loss in the discipline policy if the suspension were overruled. He was concerned that the solution might become less manageable if the mother were not calmed and if the issue were to be handled by the district office, which was a possibility if she lodged another complaint there.

Mr. Prince decided to back the authority of the assistant principal and suspend the two students. He listened to the mother and explained the situation. He was firm and fair. The effectiveness of the solution implementation was positive in relation to the school's student body and the assistant principal. Manageability of the solution implementation became easier when the district office backed his authority after the mother complained there, too. The principal thought that the solution cost of such a "small" problem was high in terms of his time. He felt that he owned the solution and its implementation. He saw no need to think of a solution monitoring design.

CASE #30

When There Is Interference With Implementing
Staff Development Plans

Mr. Richard Owens is a principal of a senior high school composed of grades 9 through 12. The school enrolls about 3,000 students. Mr. Owens has been principal of this school for the past 6 years. He has four assistant principals. Altogether he has been an administrator for a total of 16 years.

The principal was facing a problematic situation in the area of staff development. Difficulties appeared in instructional time, teacher contracts, and teacher support. The principal decided to face and participate in this problematic situation. His overall goal was to promote and enhance staff development. He was encouraged somewhat because he saw teachers spending quality time and enhancing their own satisfaction in the process. But in discussions with various groups in the school, the principal also saw the problematic issues mentioned above. He initiated extensive discussions with individuals in order to learn about the origin of the issues in this school. He also investigated the origin on his own. At the inception he saw himself, one of four assistant principals, another midlevel administrator in the school, and the department chairs as participants in and those responsible for the problematic issues. The principal considered the same three issues mentioned above as also specific problems to work on, namely: instructional time, teacher contracts, and teacher support.

At this point the principal felt that he owned these problems. These staff development problems were high on his priority list. He also considered the day-to-day requirements associated with these problems. These were somewhat lower on his priority list. Other administrators assisted him. The principal foresaw positive effects if actions were taken and negative ones if they were not. He considered the coordination phase to be somewhat difficult, but he did not see manageability difficulties in the planning phase of the project.

Mr. Owens decided that the problem to work on would be to pursue the overall staff development planning activities despite the difficulties associated with instructional time, the union, and teacher support. His strategy was to choose one item at a time, consider several solutions that might be applicable for this item, choose one solution, bring it to the planning group, and work for a consensus to adopt this solution. He pursued this strategy after extensive discussions with several individuals and groups. He felt that he owned the possible solutions. Pursuing the solutions was high on his priority list. Mr. Owens saw positive effects of the solutions if implemented. But the cost of these solutions was going to be high. It included district funds for salaries and stipends and private funds as well. The principal considered the manageability of the solutions to be satisfactory if at least 60% was accomplished. He hoped for at least that.

When the principal decided on the preferred solution to each item, he spent quite a bit of time promoting confidence in the project in those who were unconvinced. He actually sold the program to them. If he encountered unexpected and insurmountable obstacles, he used another solution, which he had conceived but did not share earlier with others. Obstacles actually appeared occasionally due to positions taken by the union, the school district office, parents, and even students. At times, the principal called for an organizational retreat, in which he tried to overcome the obstacles. He felt that the effectiveness of the solution implementation process was high; the manageability, satisfactory; and the cost, not very high at all. At this point he felt also that all of the school's administrators owned the solution implementation process. He did not believe in giving credit to himself for accomplishments at this stage of the project.

The principal decided on a design for monitoring the solution implementation process. He also implemented this design. Mr. Owens fostered feedback from all of the individuals involved. He also asked the staff and the teachers specific questions about importance, worthwhileness, and effect on "your work." The principal felt that the cost of the monitoring system was not high at all. Based on input that he solicited and on his own investigation, he found out that the monitoring effectiveness was high and that others wanted him to share the content of the results with them.

REFERENCES

Abbott, M. G. (1974). Principal Performance. In J. A. Culbertson, C. Hanson, & R. Morrison (Eds.), *Performance objectives for school principals* (pp. 196-220). Berkeley, CA: McCutchan.

Alkin, M. C., Daillack, R., & White, P. (1979). *Using evaluations: Does evaluation make a difference?* Beverly Hills, CA: Sage.

Barber, L. W. (1990). Self assessment. In J. Millman & L. Darling-Hammond (Eds.), *Teacher evaluation* (pp. 216-228). Newbury Park, CA: Sage.

Barry, J., Alkin, M. C., & Ruskus, J. (1985). Organizing evaluations for use as a management tool. *Studies in Educational Evaluation, 11,* 131-158.

Berk, R. A. (Ed.). (1981). *Educational evaluation methodology.* Baltimore, MD: Johns Hopkins University Press.

Bickel, W. E., & Cooley, W. W. (1985). Decision-oriented evaluational research in school districts: The role of dissemination processes. *Studies in Educational Evaluation, 11,* 183-204.

Bird, T. (1990). The school teacher's portfolio. In J. Millman & L. Darling-Hammond (Eds.), *Teacher evaluation* (pp. 241-256). Newbury Park, CA: Sage.

Blum, R. E., & Butler, J. A. (1985). Managing improvement by profiling. *Educational Leadership, 42*(6), 54-58.

Bolton, D. L. (1980). *Evaluating administrative personnel in school systems*. New York: Teachers College.

Borich, G. D. (1985). Needs assessment and the self evaluating organization. *Studies in Educational Evaluation, 11*, 205-215.

Boyd, W. L., & Immegart, G. L. (1979). Education's turbulent environment and problem-finding: Lines of convergence. In G. L. Immegart & W. L. Boyd (Eds.), *Problem-finding in educational administration* (pp. 275-289). Lexington, MA: Lexington Books.

Calfee, R. (1988). *Indicators of literacy*. New Brunswick, NJ: Rutgers University, Center for Policy Research in Education.

Campbell, R. E., Cunningham, L. L., Nystrand, R. D., & Usdan, M. D. (1980). *The organization and control of American schools*. Columbus, OH: Charles E. Merrill.

Castetter, W. B. (1976). *The personnel function in educational administration*. New York: Macmillan.

Cousins, J. B., & Leithwood, K. A. (1986). Current empirical research on evaluation utilization. *Review of Educational Research, 56*(3), 331-364.

Cronbach, L. J. (1963). Course improvement through evaluation. *Teachers College Record, 64*(3), 672-683.

Darling-Hammond, L., Wise, A. E., & Pease, S. R. (1983). Teacher evaluation: The organizational context. *Review of Educational Research, 53*(3), 245-328.

Deal, T. E., Neufeld, B., & Rallis, S. (1982). Hard choices in hard times. *Educational Leadership, 39*, 298-302.

DeRoche, E. F. (1987). *An administrator's guide for evaluating programs and personnel*. Boston: Allyn & Bacon.

Drake, T. L., & Roe, W. H. (1986). *The principalship*. New York: Macmillan.

Duke, D. L., & Stiggins, R. J. (1985). Evaluating the performance of school principals. *Educational Administrative Quarterly, 21*(4), 71-98.

Eisner, E. W. (1985). *The educational imagination on the design and evaluation of school programs*. New York: Macmillan.

Fawcett, C. W. (1979). *School personnel systems*. Lexington, MA: D. C. Heath.

Gally, J. (1982). *The evaluation component: An exploratory study in educational administration*. Unpublished doctoral dissertation, University of California, Santa Barbara.

Getzels, J. W. (1979). Problem-finding and research in educational administration. In G. L. Immegart & W. L. Boyd (Eds.), *Problem-finding in educational administration* (pp. 5-22). Lexington, MA: Lexington Books.

Getzels, J. W., Lipham, J. M., & Campbell, R. F. (1968). *Educational administration as a social process.* New York: Harper & Row.

Glasman, N. S. (1979). A perspective on evaluation as an administrative function in education. *Education Evaluation and Policy Analysis, 1*(5), 39-44.

Glasman, N. S. (1982). The school principal as evaluator. *Administrator's Notebook, 31*(2), 1-4.

Glasman, N. S. (1986a). *Evaluation-based leadership.* Albany: State University of New York Press.

Glasman, N. S. (1986b). Three evaluation-related behaviors of the school principal. *Educational Evaluation and Policy Analysis, 8*(3), 227-236.

Glasman, N. S., & Heck, R. (Eds.). (1992-1993). New ways to assess the performance of school principals (Pts. I & II). *The Peabody Journal of Education, 68*(1 & 2).

Glasman, N. S., & Nevo, D. (1988). *Evaluation in decisionmaking.* Boston: Klaver Academic.

Goldman, P., Dunlap, D. M., & Conley, D. T. (1993). Facilitative power and non-standardized solutions to school site restructuring. *Educational Administration Quarterly, 29*(1), 69-92.

Gorton, R. A., & Snowden, P. E. (1993). *School leadership and administration.* Madison, WI: Brown Benchmark.

Griffith, D. E. (1958). Administration as decisionmaking. In A. W. Halpin (Ed.), *Administrative theory in education* (pp. 119-149). New York: Macmillan.

Guba, E. G., & Lincoln, Y. S. (1981). *Effective evaluation.* San Francisco: Jossey-Bass.

Guthrie, J. T. (1987). *Indicators of reading education.* New Brunswick, NJ: Rutgers University, Center for Policy Research in Education.

Hanson, K. M. (1991). *Educational administration and organizational behavior.* Boston: Allyn & Bacon.

Hemphill, J. L. (1958). Administration as problem solving. In Halpin, A. W. (Ed.), *Administrative theory in education* (pp. 89-118). New York: Macmillan.

House, E. R. (1980). *Evaluating with validity*. Beverly Hills, CA: Sage.

Hoy, W. K., & Miskel, C. G. (1991). *Educational administration*. New York: McGraw-Hill.

Hunt, J., & Buser, R. L. (1977). Evaluating the principal: Partnership or paternalism? *NASSP Bulletin, 61*, 10-15.

Kimbrough, R. B., & Nunnery, M. Y. (1988). *Educational administration*. New York: Longman.

Kowalski, T. J. (1991). *Case studies in educational administration*. New York: Longman.

Kowalski, T. J., & Reitzug, V. C. (1993). *Contemporary school administration*. New York: Longman.

Lacayo, N. J. (1992). *Principals' self reported perceptions of state mandated evaluation*. Unpublished doctoral dissertation, University of California, Santa Barbara.

Leithwood, K., & Montgomery, D. (1986). *Improving principals effectiveness: The principal profile*. Toronto, Canada: Ontario Institute of Studies in Education.

Lewy, A. (Ed.). (1977). *Curriculum evaluation*. Paris: UNESCO.

Lipham, J. M., & Hoeh, J. A., Jr. (1974). *The principalship*. New York: Harper & Row.

Lunenberg, F. C., & Ornstein, A. C. (1991). *Educational administration*. Belmont, CA: Wadsworth.

McNeil, J. D. (1990). *Curriculum*. Glenview, IL: Scott, Foresman.

Millman, J., & Darling-Hammond, L. (Eds.). (1990). *Teacher evaluation*. Newbury Park, CA: Sage.

Murphy, J., Hallinger, P., Peterson, K. D., & Lotto, L. S. (1987). The administrative control of principals in effective school districts. *The Journal of Educational Administration, 25*(2), 61-73.

Oliva, P. F. (1982). *Developing the curriculum*. Boston: Little, Brown.

Parkay, F. W., & Hall, G. E. (1992). *Becoming a principal*. Boston: Allyn & Bacon.

Patton, M. C. (1978). *Utilization-forward evaluation*. Beverly Hills, CA: Sage.

Patton, M. I. (1982). *Practical evaluation*. Beverly Hills, CA: Sage.

Popham, W. J. (Ed.). (1974). *Evaluation in education*. Berkeley, CA: McCutchan.

Scriven, M. (1967). The methodology of evaluation. *AERA monograph series in curriculum evaluation* (No. 1). Chicago: Rand McNally.

Scriven, M. (1973). Goal-free evaluation. In E. R. House (Ed.), *School evaluation: The politics and processes*. Berkeley, CA: McCutchan.

Sergiovanni, T. J. (1987). *The principalship*. Boston: Allyn & Bacon.

Seyfarth, J. T. (1991). *Personnel management for effective schools*. Boston: Allyn & Bacon.

Shavelson, R. F., McDonnell, L. M., & Oakes, J. (Eds.). (1989). *Indicators for monitoring mathematics and science education*. Santa Monica, CA: Rand Corporation.

Simon, H. A. (1961). *Administrative behavior*. New York: Macmillan.

Simon, H. A., & Associates. (1986). *Decisionmaking and problem solving*. Washington, DC: National Academy Press.

Sirotnik, K. A. (1987). The information side of evaluation for local school improvement. *International Journal of Educational Research*, 2(1), 70-90.

Stewart, R. (1982). *Choices for the manager*. Englewood Cliffs, NJ: Prentice-Hall.

Stoops, E., Rafferty, M., & Johnson, R. E. (1981). *Handbook for educational administration*. Boston: Allyn & Bacon.

Stufflebeam, D. L. (1971). *Educational evaluation and decisionmaking*. Bloomington, IN: POK National Study Committee on Evaluation.

Stufflebeam, D. L. (1974). Alternative approaches to educational evaluation. In W. J. Popham (Ed.), *Evaluation in education* (pp. 95-144). Berkeley, CA: McCutchan.

Stufflebeam, D. L., & Webster, W. J. (1988). Evaluation as an administrative function. In N. J. Boyan (Ed.), *Handbook of research on educational administration* (pp. 569-602). New York: Longman.

Thompson, M. S. (1980). *Benefit-cost analysis for program evaluation*. Beverly Hills, CA: Sage.

Ubben, G. C., & Hughes, L. W. (1987). *The principal*. Boston: Allyn & Bacon.

Valentine, J. W. (1992). *Effective teacher evaluation*. Boston: Allyn & Bacon.

Webb, L. D., Greer, J. T., Montello, P. A., & Norton, M. S. (1987). *Personnel administration in education*. Columbus, OH: Merrill.

Wise, A. E., Darling-Hammond, L., McLaughlin, M. W., & Bernstein, H. T. (1984). *Teacher evaluation: A study of evaluation practices*. Santa Monica, CA: Rand Corporation.

Wittrock, M. L. (1986). Student thought processes. In Wittrock, M. C. (Ed.), *Handbook of research on teaching* (pp. 297-314). New York: Macmillan.

Young, M. (1983). *Social scientist as innovator*. Cambridge, MA: Abt.

Zey, M. (Ed.). (1992). *Decision making*. Newbury Park, CA: Sage.

INDEX

Abbott, M. S., 100
Administration, 3
Administrative domains, 66-69
Administrative evaluation, 2, 39-40
Administrative issues, 12, 87, 104, 110,
    origin of, 12, 87, 104, 110
    participants in, 12, 87, 104, 110
    responsibility for, 12, 87, 104, 110
Administrative problems, 12, 87, 104, 110
    effects of, 12, 88, 105, 110
    known, 17-23
    owners of, 12, 87, 104, 110
    predicted manageability of, 12, 88, 105, 111
Administrative solutions, 12-13, 20, 89, 106, 112
    alternative, 12-13, 89, 106, 112
    cost of, 13, 21, 89, 106, 112
    effects of, 13, 21, 89, 106, 112
    manageability of, 13, 21, 83, 106, 112
    owners of, 13, 21, 89, 106, 112
Alkin, M. C., 4, 96

Barber, L. W., 102
Barry, J., 96
Berk, R. A., 6
Bernstein, H. T., 4
Bickel, W. E., 4
Bilingual classes, 40-42
Bilingual education, value of, 126-128
Bilingual master plan, 145-146
Bird, T., 117
Blum, R. E., 6
Bolton, D. L., 100
Borich, G. D., 4
Boyd, W. L., 20
Buser, R. L., 100
Butler, J. A., 6

Calfee, R., 6
Campbell, R. F., 3, 4
Castetter, W. B., 100
Combination classes, 121-123
Conley, D. T., 95
Cooley, W. W., 4
Cousins, J. B., 4
Cronbach, L. J., 6

Cunningham, L. L., 4

Daillack, R., 4
Darling-Hammond, L., 4, 5, 6
Deal, T. E., 100
Decision-evaluation relationships, 94-99
Decision-making, 7, 96-98
Decisions
    and administrative use of
        evaluation, 71-84
    and evaluation instrument, 23-29, 100-119
    and evaluation model, 9-14
De Roche, E. F., 4, 6
Detention hall, 52-54
Disabled teacher, 137-138
Drake, T. L., 8
Duke, D. L., 100
Dunlap, D. M., 95

Educational Administration Literature, 3
Eisner, E. W., 6
Enrollment uncertainties, 124-126
Evaluation, 1-3, 36
    as a political mechanism, 99
    curriculum, 5
    direct, 3-5
    externally mandated, 4, 36
    in administration, 94-96
    internal, 3-5
    kinds of, 3
    problem-based, 9
    problem-driven, 9, 36
    professional, 2, 5-7
    program, 6
    systematic, 7
    teacher, 4-5
Evaluation information, use of, 102-118
Evaluation methodologies, 14, 37, 85-91, 115, 117-118

determinants of, 85-86
Evaluation object, 6, 12-14, 87-90, 115, 117-118

Fawcett, C. W., 100

Gally, J., 12
Getzels, J. W., 3, 17, 20, 38
Gifted classes, 49-52
Glasman, N. S., 3, 4, 6, 20, 96, 100, 102, 117
Goldman, P., 95
Gorton, R. A., 94
Greer, J. T., 5, 100
Griffiths, D. E., 10
Guba, E. G., 6
Guthrie, J. T., 6

Hall, G. E., 9
Hallinger, P., 100
Hanson, K. M., 10, 11
Heck, R., 100, 102, 117
Hemphill, I. L., 10
Hoch, Jr., J. A., 9
House, E. R., 5, 13
Hoy, W. K., 8, 10, 11, 12
Hughes, L. W., 8
Hunt, J., 100

Immegart, G. L., 20
Implementation process, 13, 21-22, 89, 107, 113
    cost of, 13, 22, 89, 107, 113
    effectiveness of, 13, 22, 89, 107, 113
    manageability of, 13, 22, 89, 109, 113
    owners of, 13, 22, 89, 107, 113

Johnson, R. E., 4

Kimbrough, R. B., 65
Kowalski, T. J., 5, 22, 119

Lacayo, N. J., 4
Leithwood, K., 4, 10, 11
Lewy, A., 5
Lincoln, Y., 3, 4, 5, 6
Lipham, J. M., 3, 9
Lotto, L. S., 100
Lunenberg, F. C., 4, 11, 20

McDonnell, L. M., 6
McLaughlin, M. W., 4
McNeil, T. O., 5
Millman, J., 5
Miskel, C. G., 8, 10, 11, 12
Monitoring implementation
    cost of, 13, 23, 90, 108, 114
    effectiveness of, 13, 23, 90, 108,
        114
Montello, P. A., 5, 100
Montgomery, D., 10, 11
Murphy, J., 100

Nevo, D., 4, 96
Newfeld, B., 100
Norton, M. S., 5, 100
Nunnery, M. Y., 65
Nystrand, R. D., 4

Oakes, J., 6
Oliva, P. F., 5
Ornstein, A. C., 4, 11, 20

Parkay, F. W., 9
Patton, M. C., 6, 14
Pease, S. R., 6
Petersen, K. D., 100
Physical violence, 54-57, 61-63
Popham, W. J., 6

Problematic situations, 10, 12, 37,
    103, 109
    and administrative domains,
        66-69
    and the use of evaluation, 65-
        71, 112-113
    illustrative case of, 15-17, 17-23

Racial discrimination charges, 59-
    61
Rafferty, M., 4
Rallis, S., 100
Reitzug, M., 119
Rol, W. K., 8
Ruskus, J., 96

School
    cuts, 147-148
    image, 130-132
    leadership, 157-159
    overcrowding, 153-155
    publicity, 155-157
    restructuring, 57-59
School principals, 34-63
    assistant high, 54-59, 75, 82
    elementary, 39-49, 72-73, 78-79
    high, 59-63, 76, 83
    middle, 49-54, 74, 80-81
    ongoing thoughts and actions,
        101
Scriven, M., 6, 12
Self-assessment, 102-116
Sergiovanni, T. J., 14
Severely handicapped student,
    151-153
Seyfarth, J. T., 5
Shavelson, R. F., 6
Simon, H. A., 10, 96, 98
Sirotnik, K. A., 96
Snowden, P. E., 94
Southern California cities, 39
Staff development, 161-163
Staffing problems, 47-49

Stewart, R., 14
Stiggens, R. J., 100
Stoop, S. E., 4
Student
    attendance policy, 148-150
    demonstration, 140-141
    failure and the home, 128-130
    misbehavior, 141-143, 143-145,
        159-161
Stufflebeam, D. L., 6, 91, 96, 119

Teaching aid
    ineffective, 135-137
Teachers
    applying for a job, 42-44
    in need of improvement, 44-
        46
Thompson, M. S., 6

Ubben, G. C., 8
Usden, M. D., 4

Valentine, J. W., 5, 6

Weak teachers, 133-135
Webb, L. D., 5, 100
Webster, W. J., 119
White, P., 4
Wise, A. E., 4, 6
Wittrock, M. L., 6

Young, M., 95

Zey, M., 99